THE LAST GREAT ADVENTURE

A Novel about Heaven

To Rachel! We love you
& are so proud of our "other"
daughter! God Bless –
I Cor. 13:12

Phillip D. Wilson

[signature: Phillip D. Wilson]

CROSSLINK
PUBLISHING

The Last Great Adventure

℘ CrossLink Publishing
℘ www.crosslinkpublishing.com

ISBN 978-1-936746-40-8

For Noah and Kelsie.
"I love you more" than you will ever know;
and I fully expect to "catch up with you later."

But as it is written, Eye hath not seen, nor ear heard, neither have entered into the heart of man, the things which God hath prepared for them that love him. – 1 Corinthians 2:9 (KJV)

To die will be an awfully big adventure. – Peter Pan

CONTENTS

CHAPTER ONE 1
CHAPTER TWO 8
CHAPTER THREE 15
CHAPTER FOUR 22
CHAPTER FIVE 29
CHAPTER SIX 42
CHAPTER SEVEN 54
CHAPTER EIGHT 60
CHAPTER NINE 67
CHAPTER TEN 77
CHAPTER ELEVEN 84
CHAPTER TWELVE 93
CHAPTER THIRTEEN 100
CHAPTER FOURTEEN 106
CHAPTER FIFTEEN 112
CHAPTER SIXTEEN 119
CHAPTER SEVENTEEN 127
CHAPTER EIGHTEEN 136
CHAPTER NINETEEN 142
CHAPTER TWENTY 150
CHAPTER TWENTY ONE 159
CHAPTER TWENTY TWO 167
CHAPTER TWENTY THREE 176
CHAPTER TWENTY FOUR 185
CHAPTER TWENTY FIVE 193
CHAPTER TWENTY SIX 200
CHAPTER TWENTY SEVEN 207
CHAPTER TWENTY EIGHT 214
CHAPTER TWENTY NINE 222
CHAPTER THIRTY 228
CHAPTER THIRTY ONE 234

CHAPTER THIRTY TWO 245
CHAPTER THIRTY THREE 254
CHAPTER THIRTY FOUR 262
CHAPTER THIRTY FIVE.. 271
CHAPTER THIRTY SIX 280
CHAPTER THIRTY SEVEN 286
CHAPTER THIRTY EIGHT.. 293
CHAPTER THIRTY NINE 300
AFTERWORD... 307

INTRODUCTION

One of the greatest gifts that God ever gave me was that of being a father to two of the most exceptional children He ever created. Lindsey Jo and Noah have always been and always will be a tremendous blessing to us.

We are fortunate that Lindsey Jo and her husband Bryant, are healthy, happy and dedicated to the Lord, as well as to each other. They have been successful in life, marriage, and their spiritual walk—a rare thing in the times in which we live. Bryant is a terrific Christian man; a blessing to our daughter and our family. Lindsey Jo is an inspiration to the coaches and teens she works with as a part of the Fellowship for Christian Athletes. She is funny, talented, strong and loving. I am so proud of her. I couldn't ask for a more perfect daughter. Thank you God for lending her to us.

Noah has been a success in his life and spiritual walk as well; however, his success must be measured differently, due to the different path God has taken him on. You see, Noah and his girlfriend, Kelsie Trobaugh, left this life due to a tragic motorcycle accident on March 20, 2010. He was nearly 19; she was barely 17. The heartache and loss our families have felt cannot begin to be expressed. Suffice it to state that when others say, "I can't imagine," they are right. They can't. I have learned that those who have lost children can't even really help each other fully grasp the pain. We are all different; our relationships with our children are all unique. The best we can to is love one another and pray for one another.

Since both Noah and Kelsie were Christians that left behind a witness of a relationship with Christ, it has given us immense comfort to believe that we will see them again. As a part of that comfort, I have taken some time to write about what it might be like for them to experience Heaven, in story form. While I know that the imagination of man falls woefully short of grasping the wonders of eternity, I enjoy trying. That's what this book is all about- The Last Great Adventure. I believe that Noah and Kelsie are experiencing that adventure even as we speak.

Now I know that I will have naysayers that say I have the theology, the descriptions, the timing all wrong. For those that think so, please understand that it is with all the Christian love I can muster that I must say I do not care. One day, when we stand before God, we will all find that we have been wrong about something. On that day, if we have been blessed enough to make Heaven our home, we will not care about such trivial matters. We will only be glad to be there, in the presence of our Creator.

Others may say that I am just a deluded father, dreaming up fairy tales to console my grief. They may say there is no God, no Heaven, no life after death. For those that think that, I hope they read this book and develop a different idea about Heaven, life and Jesus Christ. And as fantastic as I hope to describe it, for Noah and Kelsie, I know that Heaven far exceeds my description. I can't wait to find out for myself.

CHAPTER ONE

We aren't like everyone here, and no one will ever see. Time will run out. But there's nothing here we must do, so let time run out so we can go home. We will live like them for a lifetime before it is done, but let us not forget who we are, me and you.

—Noah Wilson, in a letter to his sister, Lindsey Jo.

Noah Isaac Wilson was a strong young man with beautiful blue eyes, framed in long black lashes. His hair was thick and wooly, with medium brown curls that he fought to keep in check by keeping his hair cropped short and wearing a ball cap. He stood six feet tall and weighed one hundred and fifty eight pounds, very athletic, with quick reflexes and a quicker wit.

Rosy cheeked and tan, a few youthful freckles peppered the bridge of his nose, while his chin was covered by a thin but well groomed beard. His teeth formed an even, white smile, which he was quick to flash in a laugh or to charm those he came in contact with.

Noah was a musician; a self-taught drummer and guitarist that played every Sunday at the little nondenominational church his father pastored. He was extremely talented, but Noah never seemed to have the confidence to accept it. "I'm not that good," was all he would say.

Still, he loved to play a variety of music from Christian to country to progressive and classic rock.

The teen was also very artistic, often drawing cars, people, landscapes, buildings and animals with such recognition of light and perspective that many of his friends thought he should pursue a career in illustration. Several friends and co-workers asked him to design tattoos for them, and many more were permanently inked with his art after he was gone.

Noah had worked at a variety of odd jobs since he was a small boy. For the past couple of years before his high school graduation, he worked as a helper on a residential construction crew, framing and finishing houses. He enjoyed the work and was good at it, laying out rafters, building stud walls, climbing to rooftops with agility and strength that only comes from youth and skill.

For a while after his graduation, he had continued to work with the builder, while taking a night shift job with a local auto parts distributor as a forklift operator. While very intelligent, Noah found school boring and had no desire to attend college. His plan was to take a year off while working until the following spring and enter a training program to become an electrical lineman. This career paid well, and Noah thought work in "the great outdoors" appealed to him.

Until the first of that year, Noah had been in a relationship with a petite blonde named Kayla for nearly three years. She was a high school junior in the small Tennessee town where they grew up. At barely five feet tall, with long blonde hair, and fiery green eyes, this shy, beautiful country girl's attention kept Noah close, until shortly after Christmas, when he suddenly broke off the relationship. "I love her," he once said, "and I will never deny it. But we just aren't meant to be together." Then, just as quickly, Noah was drawn to a girl from a neighboring town, like a moth to a flame. At the time, his friends and family didn't know what to make of it. Everyone had assumed that given the length of their relationship, Noah and Kayla would eventually wind up getting married. Looking back, however, it was easy to see that there was a supernatural force pulling Noah and his new love interest toward a common destiny.

The girl that had captured Noah's attention was a tall, tan red head, with a sunny smile, dimples, and eyes so blue, Noah was lost in their depth. Kelsie Dawn Trobaugh was an athletic tomboy, well-practiced in soccer and basketball, full of life and full of fun. She enjoyed skeet shooting and four wheeling more than shopping or hanging out with her girlfriends. Kelsie was the kind of girl that ordered a camouflage prom dress to wear to her senior prom. That was the girl that had captured Noah's heart.

Before they went on a single date, Noah shopped the local jewelry stores until he found a stunning set of diamond earrings that cost him nearly two weeks wages and presented them to her as a gift. When Noah's dad asked him why he would do such a thing, he simply said, "She may never date me, but I never want her to forget me." He had no need to worry; she would never forget him.

Noah began spending more and more time with Kelsie. His massive four wheel drive pickup or flashy motorcycle was often seen in her driveway. Likewise, her bright green Volkswagen could be seen showing up at his work during his lunch break. They left notes on each other's cars, texted and talked on the phone at every opportunity. Noah and Kelsie seemed happier than they had ever been. It seemed that these two had been cut from the same cloth, that they had like minds and that they had fallen hard for each other.

The first weekend in March, Noah drove Kelsie up to Knoxville to see his older sister, Lindsey Jo and her husband Bryant. While there, they all attended a Brad Paisley concert together. Noah and his sister were exceptionally close, so he felt it necessary for her to approve of this new young lady in his life. While Lindsey still loved Kayla, she could see that Noah was happy, and for her, her brother's happiness was important.

On the 19th of March, the day before the first day of spring, Noah told his mom that he loved Kelsie and that he intended to spend the rest of his life with her. Little did anyone realize that they would do exactly that.

The next day was a Saturday, unseasonably warm. Noah rolled his motorcycle out of the garage late in the morning, after catching a few hours of quick sleep at a friend's house. He had put a new set of tires on his 2004 Buell Lighting, painted in pearl metallic white, with a vivid blue racing stripe and matching wheels. Until lately, the bike had been his pride and joy; but Noah suddenly expressed an urge to try to sell it or trade it for something else. His dad would recall later that Noah said, "I don't know why, but it just makes me sick to look at it." It was as if Noah had a prophetic premonition about where this machine would take him. He met a young man at noon about twenty five miles away Noah's house, that had expressed an interest in the bike due to an ad on Noah had posted online, but the prospective buyer wasn't interested, so he called his parents and rode into nearby Gallatin, Tennessee to meet them at Walmart.

Noah spent about an hour with them, walking around the store, cracking jokes, and drooling over car magazines in the front of the store. As the family left, Noah handed his parents his favorite cap, emblazoned with the logo of a defunct local tractor dealership and said, "Hang on to this for me, will you? I'll catch up with you later."

When his mom said to be careful and told him she loved him, he flashed her a big smile and said, "I love you more."

From there, Noah rode over and picked up Kelsie, taking her to a nice local Italian restaurant. As usual, he saw several people that knew him. They would later comment that the Noah and Kelsie seemed to be having a great time. From there, they went to her father's house first, and then back to her mother's house, both of whom had divorced each other a few years ago. Neither was home, and Kelsie had forgotten her keys.

Finally, Kelsie called her mother, telling her that they were going over to Noah's house to watch a movie on television. It was only three miles away. Since it was almost seven p.m. and the weather had begun to cool, Noah gave Kelsie his hoodie to keep her warm, and the two headed for his house on a small two lane side road. The sun was shining; the road was clear and dry. The two teens cruised along enjoying the last part of the day, as Kelsie leaned into Noah and held on tightly.

Meanwhile, a young man living in an apartment about a mile down the road hurried out of his front door and jumped in his car. The young man was late for work, and knew that he couldn't afford to be late. His job in as a security guard wasn't much, but he needed it to provide for his wife and two young children.

As the security guard came to end to the access road that emptied onto the street, it was unclear if he stopped at the stop sign or not. It was also unclear as to whether or not he looked both ways before he pulled out. One thing however was abundantly clear; he did not see the motorcycle that was nearly to him when he pulled out.

There was no time to stop, no opportunity to react. The police report would later say they estimated that Noah was traveling at no more than five miles over the posted speed limit, which was forty miles an hour. Noah's motorcycle struck the car in the side of the car just behind the front fender. Noah, Kelsie and the motorcycle were thrown forward, over the hood. The bike flipped out into a field on the opposite side of the road; Noah and Kelsie came to rest in a heap on the pavement.

Noah's injuries were so immediate and extensive, his heart stopped before his body hit the ground. Kelsie's helmet was thrown off by the impact, and her head juries were severe enough that she stopped breathing after a few minutes. Within moments, an ambulance was on the scene. It was already too late for Noah, and although the EMT's desperately began to treat Kelsie, she slipped away.

Every extraordinary adventure begins somewhere; Noah Isaac Wilson and Kelsie Dawn Trobaugh's epic adventure began on the last day of their mortal life . . . the first day of spring, March 20, 2010.

CHAPTER TWO

oah stood on the edge of the road. The sun was going down, but the chill that he had felt in the air a few moments ago was gone. With intense clarity, he surveyed the scene. A white midsize Chrysler was sitting sideways on the street, with the front wheels off the edge of the road, its windshield shattered, the driver sitting behind the wheel in a semiconscious stupor. He turned to look up the road and saw a mangled motorcycle lying in the edge of a grassy field about fifteen yards from where he stood. It was his bike. Plastic and aluminum bits were scattered on the road; his eyes followed the path of debris back to its origin, where he now stood.

As his eyes dropped to his own feet, Noah saw a young man lying in the road. His limbs were twisted, his white t-shirt was torn and the face shield was missing from his black full face helmet. There was almost no blood, but it was evident by the trauma to his body and the way his helmet was crushed on the left side, that this young man was dead. As he peered into the hole once covered by the face shield, he recognized the face. He had shaved it with some regularity and trimmed the short cropped beard that outlined the jaw. It was his face. The young man was him.

Before he could process that thought, he heard the sound of labored breathing . . . Kelsie. He turned suddenly and found her lying just a few feet behind him. He had undoubtedly taken the majority of the impact with his own body, but Kelsie was still in extremely poor shape. Her helmet was gone, her face was bloody and her neck looked as if it might be broken. She was fading, and Noah knew it wouldn't be long. But somehow, Noah felt at peace, for him, as well as for her. Peace had never been this complete—reality never this sharp. It was as if he had awakened from a deep sleep, suddenly and completely.

As Noah knelt beside her, Kelsie moved her hand to reach out for him. She could sense him, even if Kelsie couldn't see him. He reached out and put his hand on hers; it was cold. "Kelsie," he said, in a quiet, comforting voice. "It's okay. I'm here. We're going to be all right."

As he spoke to her, a few people were already running to the scene. This first one to them was a short, thick, middle aged woman that had run from a house just down the road, with a look of urgency, coupled with tragic sadness. She knelt by Noah's lifeless body and peered into his helmet. "Oh baby, you're already gone, aren't you?" she said, as a tear slid down her nose. The woman called to a young man in a faded black t-shirt and dirty jeans that was coming out of one of the apartments facing the accident scene. "Call 911," she shouted. To a visibly shaken girl that was standing by the edge of the road, she said, "Go to my house up there," she pointed toward the little red brick ranch style home she had just come from, "And get a sheet. Just grab the top one off the first bed you come to . . . and bring the bed spread with it." Then she was up, and turning from Noah's lifeless body, approached Kelsie.

The woman fell to her knees on the opposite side to where Noah knelt now. The tears were flowing freely now, as she took Kelsie's other hand and brushed her long straight red hair away from her face. "Stay with us sweetheart, it's gonna be okay," the woman said, trying her best to invoke a soothing, maternal tone. Noah thought to himself, it's going to be all right, but not the way you think.

Noah spoke Kelsie's name again. "You need to focus, Kelsie," he said. "I know you're hurting, but I think it's time to go. You've got to trust me. I know you love me, I know you're ready; I know you want us to be together. It's time to go. Take my hand, don't be afraid. It's going to be all right." For a long moment, Noah thought that she would have to endure minutes, maybe longer, of not breathing. Maybe she wouldn't go with him, maybe she wasn't supposed to.

Suddenly, as he watched her tall athletic frame fight to remain alive, her face cleared of blood and injury as she drew closer to him; she sat up, leaving the broken body behind, took his hand and stood as Noah helped her to her feet. "Noah, what happened?" Kelsie asked, as her deep blue eyes looked into his.

Noah drew her close as he stepped back and put his arm around her. "Well," he started slowly, "It looks like we hit that guy that pulled out in front of us. I don't know how to say this, but I think we are done. Outta here. Dead. Game over."

Kelsie looked at him, her deep blue eyes reflecting the reality that was sinking in. He knew what she was feeling; the sudden clarity of her senses, the quick twinge of panic washed away by a wave of indescribable peace. She looked around at the accident, their bodies lying in the road. "Oh Noah, you are so broken," she gasped. "And I'm still breathing."

"I never felt a thing," Noah replied. "Don't even remember the impact. And as far as your body, it's just trying to hang on, just doing what comes natural. But it won't last long. Can you feel it?" Noah inquired, curious now about both "Kelsies" existing separately; one existed physically, the other spiritually.

"No, not really. I did feel some pain before, when I was still in there. But mostly I was just numb, like when you hit your thumb with a hammer," she replied. Kelsie looked sad, and at first Noah didn't understand why. Then it hit him. She was looking at the gathering crowd, the lady that was leaning over her. The people were crying, looking on in disbelief. Some were trying to help; others were standing back from the carnage.

While they watched the girl that had been sent for a sheet ran back with a tangled wad of bed clothes in her arms. "I hope this is okay," she said to the woman that was stroking Kelsie's brow.

"That will be fine," the woman said, as she stood and took the rumpled bed spread from the girl. She covered Kelsie with it up to her shoulders to keep her warm. "Can you stay with her?" the woman asked the girl. The girl nodded as her chin quivered; her face was pale. She couldn't have been much older than either of them; maybe twenty. She stood beside Kelsie's body with a mixture of hurt and uncertainty in her face. She had never been this close to death.

The middle aged woman shook the sheet out. It was white with a small pink floral pattern. Sorry son, she thought to herself. It's not very manly, but it will keep people from staring at you. The tears that had subsided now returned and blurred her vision as she stepped over to the young man's body. She ventured on last glance into his face. She would tell his parents later that while the trauma was "significant," his expression was so peaceful, "he looked like an angel."

Noah looked at Kelsie. He could tell that she could feel the same pull that he could. "I think we need to get out of here," he said.

"Yeah, me too," Kelsie replied. "But where do we go? Or I guess I should say, how do we go?" She looked at Noah intently for a moment and then she said, "This is gonna hurt our families. I don't know how they will handle it."

"Yeah it's going to hurt them a lot. But don't think we have a choice," Noah said, nodding toward their bodies lying in the road. "There is no way I'm coming back from *that* kind of damage, and I think if you went back, you'd never be the same. Besides, I think this is way it's supposed to be, don't you?" He gave her a little smile as he reached out and took her hand.

Kelsie returned his smile and nodded. "Me too. I love you, Noah." She said as her smile reached her eyes, and woke up the dimples in her cheeks.

"I love you too, Kelsie . . . and I always will. I think I say that without any doubt. Now, as you were saying, how do we get out of here?" Noah looked around and suddenly, in the fading sunset, he saw a glimmer of brightness, as if a door was opening in front of them.

As the opening widened, a prismatic display of color played around the edges, although the light shining through the doorway was pure white. In the middle of the light, a figure stood in sharp silhouette. He was exactly whom they expected Him to be. The dark hair the beard, the white robe, familiar, but somehow, the figure was new and more real to them than they had ever imagined. He stepped to the edge of the doorway, held out His hand and simply said, "Come with me. It is time."

Noah grinned, squeezed Kelsie's hand, and said, "Ask a stupid question, huh? Let's go." As the echoes of sirens began to increase and a halo of red flashing light began to brighten the evening sky, Noah Isaac Wilson and Kelsie Dawn Trobaugh walked toward the door, toward the figure in the doorway; toward their future. They did not know what was on the other side of the doorway, but they weren't afraid. The time for fear was over, forever. They were excited and they were together. As they stepped through the door, they didn't even look back.

CHAPTER THREE

When Noah and Kelsie stepped through the doorway, there was no feeling of floating, flying, or traveling anywhere. They literally stepped through from one side of the opening to the other. There was a strange sensation however. Although they had been outdoors when the accident occurred, stepping through the doorway felt like stepping from the *inside* to the *outside*, onto the lush thick grass on top of a beautiful green mountainside. As their eyes adjusted to the brightness, they could see that the white light was the same type of brightness one associates with stepping out of a dark room into the sunshine. What had seemed like a purely white world was alive with color. The deep green of the mountains, the intense deep blue of a cloudless, sunless sky, a myriad of flowers in a rainbow of colors swaying gently in the breeze, was almost sensory overload. It was breathtakingly beautiful.

The mountains were larger than anything either of them had ever seen or even dreamed of. While some were capped with snow, others seemed to be green all the way to the top, like the one they were standing on. The height and grandeur of scale was beyond comprehension. These mountains were, in fact, a stunning two hundred times the height of the Himalayas. They were many times the height of the atmosphere of Earth, yet Noah and Kelsie breathed easily in the crisp fresh air, as they took in the scope and breadth of this land's wonder.

As Kelsie and Noah looked across the panorama of beauty, they could see that the mountain range formed a valley of immense size, spanning millions of square miles. While they could not see the other side, they would later discover that the range they were standing on formed a complete circle around the basin. But the focal point that drew their attention was in the middle of this basin, and it was incredible.

A walled city sat in the middle of the basin, with walls so high, it made the city appear to be cubic in dimension. The walls themselves were incredibly high; higher than the surrounding mountains, and were made of transparent stone that ranged in hue from red, to blue, to yellow, to green. Although Noah and Kelsie had never seen this stone before, they recognized it as millions of cubic feet of a semiprecious stone called jasper. From where they stood looking at one of the corners of the city, they could not see the opposite end of either wall. They were looking at a single city that covered more area than half the United States.

It was all was overwhelming. "This," Noah breathed, with wonder in his voice, "Is Heaven."

Kelsie broke into a peal of joy filled laughter. "Ya think?" she teased. "Well, don't just stand there . . . let's go!" she shouted.

As they made their way down the mountain, they watched birds soar above, while butterflies danced through the flowers that dotted the landscape. This delighted Noah, because even though he had always been a "guy's guy", he loved butterflies and thought they were incredibly beautiful. While moving along, they continued to be amazed at the scale of this place. It was bigger than life . . . which made sense when they thought about it. It wasn't just bigger than life, it was beyond life.

The mountains were anchored with trees of immense size and age. What seemed like giant redwoods at first, were in fact maples, oaks, poplar and ash. Even the dogwoods were straight and tall, displaying blooms of pink, white and even yellow and blue on the same tree. It was as if these trees had grown for thousands of years with no storm, disease or pestilence to damage them. But it was more than that. These trees had grown out of soil that was not cursed by the presence of sin and death. That explained their impressive stature.

There were fruit trees too; apples, pears, dates, every type of citrus that they recognized and a dozen varieties they did not. They all simultaneously had blossoms and ripe fruit at the same time. Kelsie pulled a couple of pink, shiny fruits the size of a softball from a nearby tree and handed one to Noah. "Careful," he joked. "I think this is how Adam got into trouble in the first place." Kelsie smacked him playfully on the arm. He smelled the fruit and found it to have an almost floral fragrance. When he bit into it, he found the flesh of the fruit to be crisp like an apple, but with a flavor that was a mixture of banana and peach. "Very cool," he mumbled, with a mouthful of fruit. Bowing deeply, he said with a grin and an exaggerated flourish, "My compliments to the fruit picker." As they both enjoyed their snack, they continued to hike down the mountain at a leisurely pace.

Looking through the tops of trees along the lower parts of the mountain range, they saw movement; people. There were thousands of people making their way slowly down the gently sloping mountains. From their vantage point, they could follow the stream of people as they stepped out of nowhere onto the peaks of the nearby slopes and began to descend toward the city. "Plenty of new arrivals," commented Kelsie. "It almost makes you wonder how there would be enough room for everyone."

Noah considered this for a moment and then answered her. "Well, for one thing, Heaven is obviously huge. For another, it's not like we need to grow food, build things or make clothes. Everything we need is already here and plentiful. When you don't have to have room for factories, schools, businesses, farms . . . ." his observation trailed off as the truth of it sunk in.

"No hospitals," Kelsie continued.

"Yeah, and no prisons or funeral homes."

"No banks, no malls, no airports."

Noah nodded, "And strangely enough, no churches."

"Really?" Kelsie asked incredulously.

Noah looked at her. "No need. We're already here. The Bible says that there is no temple in the city, because God dwells with us. Besides, you already knew the answer to that, right?"

Kelsie nodded, with a new realization. "You know, now that you mention it, since we've been here, there isn't anything about all of this I've wondered about that I didn't already know the answer to. I didn't know anything about trees when I was . . . well, I mean before, but I can name them all now. That fruit we just ate is called a *dvash*, which is Hebrew for honey. It doesn't even exist on Earth, but I recognized it, knew its name . . . and even knew what it would taste like before I ate it."

Noah agreed, "Me too. It's like we suddenly know everything we need to know. No mysteries left. Any questions that come to our mind, we already have the answers."

"Kinda blows the mind, doesn't it?" Kelsie replied.

Noah gave her a malicious smile. "Takes the fun of Trivial Pursuit, that's for sure. Not that it was ever fun to begin with. Hallelujah! No more board games!" he said laughing. He had never been a fan of game night around the house, or "lame night" as his mom liked to call it.

His mom. She had to be hurting, Noah thought suddenly. It didn't really make him sad, but he was . . . concerned. He knew his dad was pretty tough; he knew that Lindsey Jo and her husband Bryant could lean on each other, but he was concerned about his mom.

Noah and his mother had grown closer over the past several months, and had enjoyed spending time together whenever possible. His mom had quit her job during the previous fall after battling depression following the death of her father in October. That time had been difficult, but it helped Noah and his mother to work on their relationship.

He had always felt a strong connection with his mother and suspected that they shared a lot in common. Noah's mom had struggled with bipolar disorder throughout his childhood, and during the past couple of years, Noah's personal bouts with significant moods swings had led to him to secretly fear that he might also be manic depressive. The positive part of all this was that since he worked an evening shift, and his mother had spent the past few months at home, they had enjoyed lunch together, worked around the house, talked and opened up to each other about many things. Now, after all she had been through, Noah's mom would have to deal with the loss of her son.

I wish there was some way I could get a message to her and let her know I'm all right, Noah thought to himself. *If I could just get Cory or somebody to go to her and tell her.* Then, suddenly, as soon as the thought came to him, Noah stepped into a vision of the night he died.

CHAPTER FOUR

Cory McClain had been Noah's best friend since they were eight years old. They had played little league baseball together, and even after they began to pursue other interests, Noah and Cory had continued to be like brothers to each other. Over the years, Cory had grown into a big man, four or five inches taller than Noah and outweighing him by seventy pounds. But as big and strong as he was, Cory's heart had remained gentle and tender. That's what everyone, including Noah, loved about him.

These young men had spent a lot of time in each other's homes, and had encouraged each other through issues with school, family, friendships, career choices, and relationships.

During Cory's senior year, he had fallen for a strong, fiery young woman named Tasia. The attraction was so strong that when Cory turned eighteen, he moved out and rented a small house with her, against his parent's wishes. He had worked every hour he could at a local fast food restaurant, trying to balance his new found responsibility with school and work, when they discovered that Tasia was pregnant with Cory's child.

This event solidified a decision that Cory had been mulling over for some time. As he finished his senior year of high school, Cory decided that he would joint the Navy, and with salary and benefits that would come from that position, he could provide for his child, and hopefully, Tasia. Their relationship had been strained by financial pressures and with a baby on the way, they had many struggles. But Cory loved Tasia, and he knew that he loved the baby that was soon coming.

During all this, Noah and Cory stayed close, with Noah coming by to check on them and offering Cory all the support he could. When Cory told Noah of her pregnancy, Noah looked him in the eye and said, "You know you've got to do the right thing by her, right?" It was more of a statement than a question, but Cory nodded just the same. Cory was raised in a small General Baptist church, and had a background very similar to Noah's. He knew that Noah's expectation was for him to marry Tasia, and take care of her and his child. He also knew that it was plainly the right thing to do. His parents had often struggled to make a living for him and his two sisters, and at times, Cory had thought he wanted no part of the frustration and weariness he had seen in his own father's eyes. But ultimately, he understood that being there for your family was part of what it meant to be a man.

Still, Cory and Tasia put off the wedding until their daughter was born. Noah still came by frequently, and sometimes just hung out with them, watching TV and talking after he and Cory had gotten off work late at night. Noah loved the infant that Tasia had given birth to. Her name was Lily, and Noah held her as if she were made of fine china.

Cory shipped off to basic training at Lake Michigan the end of February; he and Tasia made plans to marry when he returned. Cory told Noah, "Dude, you know I want you to be my best man", to which Noah replied with a cocky grin, "What are you taking about? I AM the best man." Unfortunately for Cory and unbeknownst to him, Noah had other places to be.

Cory was at basic training on the fateful day when Noah and Kelsie died. His family tried to get word to him about his best friend's death, but since they were not immediate family, the military would not allow him to receive information that was deemed as detrimental to his training. Therefore, it was not until he received a letter from his grandmother nearly two weeks later that he learned the fateful news. He called his mother, who cried with him over the phone. Cory was nearly inconsolable; the two had been closer than brothers. They had shared dreams and secrets together; theirs was an uncommonly strong friendship for two young men.

It was this bond that caused Cory several nights later to dream about Noah and the accident. It was also this bond that allowed Noah to enter into Cory's dream and speak to him one more time.

After a typically tiring day of rigorous training, Cory went to bed early and fell into a deep sleep. Sometime during that night, he suddenly found himself in a very vivid dream, seemingly wide awake and alert, standing on the edge of College Street in the dusk of the afternoon. The scene was crowded with bystanders and emergency vehicles, and he felt the pulsing red, blue and yellow lights burn into his retinas and his mind. He knew exactly where he was. A white Chrysler was sitting in the middle of the road, with a shattered windshield and a deployed air bag sagging out of the steering wheel like a pale, tired mushroom. There were two forms covered with sheets on the pavement. The faces of bystanders showed shock, grief and tears. He recognized Bo Grimes, Keith Jaeger and Mary Jarrod, friends he had went to school with. They didn't see him. He was only dreaming after all. Dreaming about the night Noah died.

When Noah was pulled back onto the scene of the accident, a number of things didn't seem quite right. It was darker, later in the evening than when he had left. Many more people were gathered. An ambulance was there, several police cars, a fire and rescue truck. His body and Keslie's were both covered with sheets. It all had a dreamlike quality; there were people standing around crying that he knew, but it all seemed so fuzzy, so indistinct.

That was when Noah spotted him. He was clearly out of place, standing out in a cacophony of noise and confusion. Cory McClain was standing to the side, taking it all in with a look of shock and grief on his face. He was dressed in a light blue shirt, with navy slacks; his Navy uniform, Noah realized. The truth of it struck him. This wasn't real; it was some kind of dream. Evidently, when he had thought of Cory, he had been able to enter this dreamlike state where he could see his friend. He had thought of getting his friend to contact his mother and suddenly, here he was.

About the time that Noah had processed what was going on, Cory spotted him standing across the road. Noah wasn't injured; in fact, he looked great. Noah was standing in front of him in a crisp white t-shirt and jeans, with his hands in his pockets and a sad little smile on his face. He walked casually across the road, around the small knot of policemen deep in discussion over the accident scene. Cory was overwhelmed by the sight of his friend. "Are you OK?" Cory asked him, looking at him in disbelief.

The emotion of the moment got the better of Noah. Tears slid down his ruddy cheeks. "Yeah, Cory, I'm fine. I'm going to be OK." He knew this was the last time he would see Cory before they met again in Heaven. A lump grew in his throat.

Cory just stared in amazement, "Are you sure?" was all he could think of to say. Noah was dead; he knew that. Yet here he was big as life.

Somehow, Corey knew that he was dreaming. But Noah standing here was just so . . . real.

Noah grinned. "Yeah, Cory, where I'm going, I'm going to be fine." Then, clearer still than anything in this dreamlike state, he heard a voice distinctly say, *Noah, it's time to go.* By the look on Cory's face, he heard the voice as well. It was God; and time for getting the message through this dream was running out.

"I understand," Noah replied, looking away into the distance. "Just give me one more minute." Noah then looked intently at Cory and put his hand on his shoulder. Noah grip was surprisingly warm and firm in the chill air. "You've got to do something for me, Cory."

Cory met his gaze. "Anything man, you know that."

Noah nodded. "You've got to take care of my mom. This is really going to hurt her. You've got to let her know I'm OK. Will you do that?"

"Noah, you know I will."

"Good," Noah said, pulling Cory into a hug. "Take care, man. I got to go. I'll see you later." Then Noah turned, walked across the road and vanished, just as Cory awoke with tears in his eyes.

Corey called his mother that morning and tearfully related his dream to her, asking about Noah's parents. When he came home, he sat in the

Wilson's living room and told them the story as he, Tasia, and Noah's parents all had a good long cry.

Tasia and Cory were married by Noah's father a few short weeks later. When asked to say something about Noah during their wedding ceremony, Noah's dad tried to convince them otherwise. "This is your day," he said. "I know he would have wanted to be here, but don't you want to focus on your day?"

Tasia insisted, however. She said, "Noah is a big part of how we got to where we are." So the couple was married in a little country church, with little Lily in her grandmother's arms on the front row.

Phil Wilson's eyes grew misty as he began the service. After Tasia's father gave her away, Noah's father took a moment to honor the couple's wishes. "As honored as Cory and Tasia is to have Chase Pitt stand with Cory today, it was their original plan for Cory's best friend Noah to be his best man at this wedding. God however, had other plans for Noah. It is Cory's and Tasia's wish to let you know that Noah was a big part of their lives and that they wish he could be here today," he stopped and swallowed the lump in his throat, before adding with a smile, "and so do I."

CHAPTER FIVE

Noah found himself standing in exactly the same place on the mountainside as he was before his excursion back to the other side. Nothing had changed; in fact Kelsie was in mid-sentence about a particularly gorgeous flower she had seen that changed from vivid yellow to a deep crimson when touched. She had not noticed that he was gone, and from the appearance of things, Noah had come back the exact instant he left.

When Kelsie turned to Noah, expecting a reaction to what she was saying, she saw the puzzled look on his face. "What's wrong?" she asked.

Slowly, Noah's quizzical expression disappeared as he broke into a grin. "I think I just did something I didn't have any idea we could do." He then explained to Kelsie how he had been concerned about his mother, and how he had thought about Cory being able to tell her he was okay. "As soon as I thought it, I stepped into one of his dreams. I was able to communicate with him. It was a real connection; I know it was. I could just tell." He went on to tell her about being at the accident site, the brief conversation with his friend and the voice that had called him back. "No sooner than I left, I was back. In fact, it was just like I never left."

Kelsie nodded. "I think you came back the same second you left. That's why I never saw anything." She pondered what Noah had said for a moment, and suddenly her eyes sparkled with a thought. "Do you think we can pass back and forth as we please? Do you think we can appear to others on the other side?" As wonderful as this place was, she was excited at the thought of being able to communicate with friends and family whenever she wanted.

Noah thought about what Kelsie said, and shook his head. "I don't think so. If people did that, we would have seen them all our lives. People on the other side couldn't get anything done without the 'dearly departed' dropping by to say hi," he replied. He suddenly became very conscious of how he and Kelsie had both come to refer to their former life as 'the other side' and how nonchalantly he had referred to them as the 'dearly departed'.

"Then how do you explain what just happened to you?" she inquired. "You think you get a special hall pass just because you are Noah Wilson?"

"Well, yeah! You know it," he replied with and exaggerated air. Then he paused. "Actually, I don't know how that happened. Maybe it was just a fluke."

Kelsie picked one of the color changing flowers she had been admiring and placed it in her hair. "Maybe we can just do it sometimes. And maybe not directly, either; just through a dream or something like that."

"That makes sense," Noah replied. "Maybe Cory was already dreaming about me, and it gave me the place to contact him. But how would he have had that dream at the instant I thought about him?"

"Maybe he didn't. Maybe you stepped into his dream days or even months later. I've got a feeling that time doesn't work the same way, or even mean anything here," Kelsie said. "We could have been here for hours, while it's been years on the other side."

Noah agreed. "I think you're right. But I'm not sure that even covers it. Not only does time mean nothing here, I think we are *outside* time. I think time is a measurement for what life *was* for us, not what it is *now*. I don't think we are limited by it anymore. Think about it for a minute; how long have we been here? I mean, we've been heading down the mountain toward the city for a while, but has it been hours, minutes or days? Already it feels more like home than where we came from."

"That's because THIS is where we came from," Kelsie said emphatically. "Don't you feel that? I never really thought about it before, but I was always a stranger over there. This is where I belong. This is home. It is all new, but at the same time, it's all familiar. I always felt loved; I had plenty of family and friends. I loved the sports, the hanging out, even the high school drama . . . sometimes. But this is it. This is where I belong."

Noah thought about words he had once written to his sister when he was about fifteen. *Let time run out so we can go home.* He had known he didn't belong. He and his sister had both had a deep, special bond, and as such, he knew that she didn't belong either. He had tried to convey as much in a letter written to her, but in the way of an overly melodramatic teenager, he had overplayed it. Lindsey Jo had brushed it aside for that reason. But they were different, and now he understood why. "You're right. We came from here to begin with. We were created for this," Noah said, opening his arms and gesturing to the splendor around them. "We're home."

Noah and Kelsie reached an outcropping of rock on the mountainside that extended outward perhaps a half mile, creating a broad flat table of granite that ran horizontally along the mountain for several miles in each direction. The rock appeared to be pink granite, shot through with wide veins of turquoise, causing a tiger stripe effect in the stone they stood on. Simple white daisies grew from cracks in the rock, providing an accent for the deep hues of the table top.

While surveying the progress of their journey, Kelsie noticed a woman descending the mountain about three hundred yards to their left. As she reached the stone floor of the outcropping, Kelsie called out to her and waved. The woman returned her greeting with a wave and a shout. She walked easily and smoothly toward them, with a grin that could be seen by the time she had covered half the distance between them.

Noah looked at Kelsie. "Never meet a stranger, do you?" She smiled and replied, "Look who's talking. You talked to my family and friends just like you had known them all your life. My grandmother thought that was one of the coolest things about you."

Noah laughed. "Well, my dad always said some of the best friends you'll ever have, you haven't met yet. And I guess even now, that's still true." Putting his arms around Kelsie, he turned to face the woman that was almost to them.

She was a young black woman, with large dark eyes, a neat, close cropped afro, and smooth, milk chocolate colored skin. She wore a clean, simple cotton dress with a small floral print. Noah guessed that it was typical of what she would have worn on the other side, since he and Kelsie had found themselves in t-shirts and jeans when they stepped through. As she approached, the woman said, "Hey there! Are ya'll angels, or are ya'll pilgrims?" Noah and Kelsie both chuckled at the thought of being angels, as well as the old fashioned use of the term 'pilgrims'.

Kelsie answered. "I guess we're pilgrims. The only people that ever called me an angel were my parents, and I don't think Noah was ever been accused of being one himself. I'm Kelsie, by the way." She stuck out her hand.

The woman gave out a throaty chuckle. "Don't give me that hand. I want a hug," the woman replied wrapping her arms tightly around Kelsie. "We are all brothers and sisters here, and I hug my family. I'm Tilly," the woman said as she turned from Kelsie and grabbed Noah in the same tight embrace.

"I'm Noah," he replied. "Where are you from, Tilly? You sound southern, like us."

"Well, if you're talkin' about the other side, I'm from Mississippi. A little wide place in the road called Deeson, in Bolivar County, over by the river. What about ya'll?" Tilly inquired.

"We're from Tennessee," Kelsie replied. "He's from Portland and I'm from White House. They're little towns just north of Nashville, up close to the Kentucky state line."

Tilly nodded in acknowledgement. "I got a sister that lives in Louisville. I've been through Nashville a couple of times when I went to see her." She processed the idea of Noah and Kelsie being from neighboring towns. "Ya'll came over together, didn't you? Too much of a coincidence for both of you to be together over here and living so close over there." She gestured as if indicating a place over the mountains.

Kelsie looked at Noah, obviously not wanting to describe the accident. Noah answered her quietly, almost reverently. "We were on a motorcycle together, and someone pulled out in front of us. There was no way to stop. I went first, and stayed around for her." He squeezed Kelsie's hand.

Tilly looked at them with a bitter sweet smile. "So ya'll were an item, huh? I can see it in the way you look at each other."

"Yeah, we were," Kelsie said. "We hadn't been together for long. But it just felt right, you know? We just fit together somehow."

Noah was lost in thought about the subject. "I had just told my mom that I wanted to marry Kelsie. I had a lot of plans . . . but I guess plans change."

"Changed for the best, I guarantee," Tilly replied. "Being married ain't never nothing but a struggle. The money problems, the kids, the worries about somebody trying to come around and tear up your family. Ya'll don't ever have to worry about that. Ya'll can spend all the time together you want to and never worry about any of that stuff."

Kelsie smiled. "I suppose you're right. I would have loved to be a mom and a wife, but I know it's tough. Maybe it's better this way." Noah pulled her close and gave her a gentle peck on the check.

"So it sounds like ya'll are pretty young," Tilly said, trying to change the subject. She had hit close to home for them, and knew this wasn't a place for sadness over the unfulfilled dreams of the other side.

"Well, yeah," Noah replied. "I guess we are. I would have been nineteen in a couple of weeks, and Kelsie is just a little over seventeen."

Tilly was taken aback. "Ya'll were just babies. I mean, I know we're all better off to be here, but ya'll were taken awful quick."

Kelsie looked at the young woman with a puzzled expression. She didn't look much older than them. But the way she talked, she sounded older. The age wasn't in her voice; it was in her words, her mannerisms. Finally, she expressed her thoughts, as tactfully as she could. "Tilly, you don't look much older than us. Can I ask how old you are?"

Tilly laughed loud and long. "Honey, I was eighty-four last August. Eighty-four! My man passed seven years ago and I've been livin' in a nursing home for two and a half years. They put me to bed last night, turned out the light, and I woke up on top of this mountain. I jumped and shouted so loud that old Saint Pete himself could probably hear me, if he's standing down yonder at that gate," she grinned, indicating the valley below. "Everybody that loves me over there is glad I got to go home, and everybody that loves me over here is gonna be glad I am home. It don't get no better than that. I feel like I'm twenty, only better. I don't think I ever felt this good."

"Us neither," Kelsie agreed. "We've been coming down the mountain at a steady pace, but the only reason we've stopped was to enjoy the surroundings. There's been no need to rest."

"I haven't even broken a sweat," Noah added. "Speaking of which, are you ladies ready to keep on traveling?"

Tilly looked at him, "Are you both okay with me traveling with you?"

Kelsie answered with a big smile. "Plenty of room for another pilgrim in this party," she said.

Noah, Kelsie and Tilly stepped to the edge of the pink granite mesa and looked down the sheer bluff that extended nearly a thousand feet before trailing off to a gentle grassy slope again. The surface was irregular with some areas that might be potential hand holds, but the way looked quite steep and difficult.

"So how to you suppose we get down from here?" Kelsie asked, looking at Noah. "You're always the big daredevil in the bunch."

Noah shot her a sardonic look. "And you see where that's got me. Besides, I don't think I get to be any kind of devil, 'dare' or otherwise over here. Oh snap! I guess that means you can't be a White House Blue Devil anymore either," he teased her.

"Okay, you two," Tilly admonished in a slightly maternal tone. "Quit playing around, now. How are we going to get down there? I'm in better shape than I've ever been, but I ain't never been a mountain climber."

"No better time than the present to start," Noah replied. "It can't be that dangerous. After all, what are you going to do, die? Been there, done that, not doing it again," he stated simply, and sat down on the edge of the pink and turquoise outcropping, with his legs hanging over. Then suddenly, he turned, and lowered himself easily down the rock face. He reached below to find a hand hold and the rock gave beneath Noah's touch to form a smooth lateral slot just the right size for his fingers. His hand slid into the slot, and he lowered himself, kicking at the stone with his foot. The same thing happened, forming a pocket that was just the right size to bear his weight. "Check it out," Noah called to the others. "You can just climb right down. The hand and foot holds just appear where you need them."

Observing Noah's lead, Kelsie and Tilly followed suit by gingerly climbing over the edge of the rock face and making their way to the grassy slope below. Tilly went much slower than her new found companions at first, out of needless caution that came from years of experience with an older, weaker body. At one point she wondered what would happen if she fell. She suspected she would have been fine, but she didn't really want to find out.

Noah thought about the way that the stone reacted to his touch as he descended. To say that it *gave* to his touch wasn't quite correct. It was more like the stone *submitted* to them as they climbed down. It was as if the rock anticipated what they wanted to accomplish and moved the way each of them needed it to. Where Tilly had wondered what a fall would have been like, Noah considered what a jump would have been like. He didn't think it would have injured him, but like Tilly, he didn't risk it. Besides, it may have been difficult to land gracefully without rolling down the slope.

By the time they reached the bottom, they were practically racing. Kelsie had reached the bottom first; her long, lanky frame working to her advantage. As she had gained confidence coming down the cliff face, she had turned in mid climb and finished the descent head first. When she got within ten feet of the bottom, she back flipped off the rock and landed lightly on her feet. Tilly was a few seconds behind her having enthusiastically passed Noah half way down. "Now you're just showing off," Tilly said to Kelsie. "You must have been some kind of basketball player."

Kelsie looked at her surprised. "How did you know I played basketball?" she asked.

"You got the look and the moves," Tilly said with a chuckle. "Besides, ain't no girl that's nearly six feet tall, and built like you are goin' to slide by the attention of a high school coach."

Kelsie blushed at the compliment. She had been quite an athlete in school, playing every sport she could, but concentrating on soccer and especially basketball. She was an aggressive and competitive player, having been known for 'checking' other players with some regularity when they guarded her too closely. This had been cause for somewhat frequent fouls, but it gained her quite a reputation. Kelsie was a force to be reckoned with, on or off the court or field. Now she was capable of far more than she had ever been able to do on the other side. She could feel it, she could sense it. She was anxious to test the limits of a limitless existence.

Noah had given up on trying to compete with Tilly and Kelsie as they rapidly descended the cliff. He had instead swung from hand to hand easily, slowly coming down the rock, enjoying the sensation of strength and control. He had turned in mid-climb and hung there a few times with his back to the stone, feeling its coolness on his skin and surveying the view of the valley as it reached out to the city wall miles ahead.

The slope below them gently fell away into dense patches of forest. The trees were assorted of every variety, and Noah noted that some appeared to be nut trees, like pecan, walnut, chestnut, as well as a half dozen types of nuts that didn't exist on the other side. Somewhere in the branches below, he could hear the sound of water. There must be a stream hidden from view nearby. Looking down, he saw the girls below, still a hundred feet from where he was. *This isn't too bad*, he thought. *I think I'll jump from here.*

"Look out below!" Noah cried, as he pushed off the rock face and performed a graceful swan dive toward the grassy slope below. Kelsie let out a startled cry as she looked up, eyes wide, just in time to see him plunging toward her. She pushed Tilly in the opposite direction and she leaped backward, unsure of what to do.

Noah hit the grass between them feet first, bending his knees into the landing, and tipping forward onto his palms, using his momentum to flip himself into a handstand. He held it for a moment before pushing off and back flipping onto his feet, gesturing with a broad sweep of his arms. "Ta-daaaa!" he said with a flourish.

Kelsie ran forward and smacked him on the chest. "I'll 'ta-da' you! You scared the daylights out of me! That wasn't funny!" she said, with a tone that wasn't quite fear or anger, but mixed with a bit of both.

"Hey now," Noah held up his hands in defense. "I was just having a little fun. I figured that would be pretty easy to do. I would have jumped from farther up, but I didn't know how I would land."

"Well if you two young'uns are through playing," Tilly said, "Maybe we can check out the forest. Maybe it's just my imagination, but I feel a little hungry. Thirsty too. I'd like to see what's around for the picking."

Noah and Kelsie both grinned sheepishly. "Yes ma'am," Noah said, and the three wandered across the grassy clearing into the trees.

CHAPTER SIX

T he trees provided an unusual perspective of shade. Since the entire land had its own radiant ambience, the shade was muted by the fact that there was a significant amount of light coming from beneath the branches, as well as the sky above. It was not as noticeable when they had been primarily in the open, but now that they had entered a wooded area, they all noted it, and commented on the phenomenon.

Tilly put it best. "It's like God knew that Heaven wouldn't be the same without a little shade now and then, so He kept it, even though He didn't have to." Noah and Kelsie agreed, since the laws of light and shadow didn't seem to apply where they were. With his artistic eye, Noah especially noticed how that the shadows and shade appeared to have an energy of their own, rather than just be caused by the absence of light.

The other thing that they noticed was that grass and wildflowers completely covered the forest floor. There were no leaves on the ground. None ever fell. What did occur however, was that a gentle rolling of colors filtered through the canopy of branches as leaves slowly turned the fiery reds, yellows and oranges of autumn and brightened back into a deep green without ever shriveling into the dead brown that came with a dip into freezing temperatures. While there was snow on the tops of some mountains, these trees would never bare their branches for the bitter chill of winter.

The group came to a small rise and when they topped it, they found the source of the water they had heard from above. A spring shooting a geyser of water a dozen feet in diameter emptied tens of thousands of gallons of water per second into a wide pool that in turn flowed into a large stream on the opposite side from where they stood. The spring head rose several feet above the level of the pool, but the width of the basin was substantial enough that they could easily see their reflection in the edges of the pool.

Tilly looked at her reflection with awestruck wonder. Unlike Noah and Kelsie, whose appearance was largely unchanged except for the absence of acne or imperfections, Tilly had not seen this face in more than sixty years. Gone were the wrinkles, the skin pocked with age spots and scars. Gone were the thinning tufts of gray hair and the flaking dry patches of scalp that had plagued her for over twenty years. The woman that smiled back at her from pool, was young, beautiful and vibrant, with perfect skin, thirty-two sparkling teeth, clear dark eyes with no dull cataracts, a lush head full of tight black curls. She ran her hand over a smooth, high cheek, and noticed her hand for the first time. The skin on the back of the hand was thick and supple; no knotted veins marred its surface, no arthritis twisted the joints beneath

43

the surface. She was more than young again; she was better than she had ever been.

It was then that she looked at her left hand to see if the scar was still there. It was, surprisingly; not as pronounced, but a faint shadow of the thick keloid scar she had carried from her youth was still there. It ran across the web between her thumb and forefinger, like a faint crescent moon, marking a deep wound that slashed through her hand.

When Tilly was thirteen, her father had come home on a fateful Saturday night in a drunken rage. Drinking binges like this were frequent for him; and when he came in as a roaring, angry tornado of a man, her mother often received the brunt of his tirades. That night, he had pushed Tilly's mother, and caused her to knock a pitcher from the table, breaking it into large heavy chunks of glass. Cursing about her carelessness, he picked up the largest piece, still attached to the handle of the pitcher and swiped it at his wife's face. Thirteen year old Tilly ran to protect her mother and threw her hand up in defense; the force of her father's fury nearly removed the girl's thumb. Horrified and suddenly sobered by his actions, Tilly's father stumbled into the night with tears of guilt stinging his face. Her mother snatched Tilly up quickly, pressed her apron to the wound until the bleeding subsided, and carefully sewed the wound back together with thick cotton thread and a large curved needle. Both mother and daughter gritted their teeth through the pain of the procedure, breathing deeply, steadily in rhythm, never uttering a word to each other.

Two things came from Tilly's action; her mother was saved from a disfiguring and possibly life threatening injury and her father never touched a drop of alcohol again. Tilly had borne the scar throughout her life and her thumb had never quite worked the way it was supposed to again. But she had come to carry the scar with a sense of pride, knowing what her sacrifice had done for both her parents.

Now the thumb worked perfectly, as she wiggled it with ease, but the faint trace of a scar was still there. Then in a sudden revelation, Tilly understood. *If Jesus still carries His scars,* she thought, *it only makes sense for me to carry mine.*

Noah broke her train of thought as he ran his hand through his closely cropped beard and noted a difference. "Cool, no more pimples," he said, admiring his now flawless skin. Adolescence had never plagued him too heavily with acne, but he had always had a problem with a few persistent bumps at his jaw line, where he factitiously groomed his fine, brown whiskers.

Kelsie beamed at the glowing, dimpled face that she saw in the pool as well. "Wow, I'm perfect. I guess nothing's changed," she quipped with an impish laugh, causing Noah to shoot her a look and scoop up a handful of water, splashing her and taking her breath with its icy freshness. She chased Noah, trying unsuccessfully to shove him into the water. He darted back and forth until finally, they fell on the grass together in a giggling heap.

"Ah, young love," Tilly said wistfully. "You don't know how good you got it. All of the good and none of the bad. No jealousy, no problems . . . not even any sexual tension. That's all gone now, and good riddance. There are plenty of things that are good about the other side, but I ain't never gonna miss the "stuff" that messes up the human relationship."

Noah and Kelsie sat up on the grass and quieted, listened to her. Kelsie's expression changed. "This is all so different for you, isn't it? I mean, you have lived for many years and now you have this great young body with all those years of experience. I've never thought that much about it before, but can I ask you something? What was getting old like?" The look in Kelsie's eyes reflected curiosity and something else, something like missed opportunity. Noah was staring at her intently, his attention rapt as well on their young-yet-old traveling companion.

Tilly's lips pursed in a small smile and she dropped her eyes and thought about it. "What a question. Ya'll are like Peter Pan or somethin'. Never knew what is was like to get old; never will know. What a blessing. Your folks are probably crying bitter tears for you, but if they thought about it, they would have cried more on the day you were born, and shouted on the day you died."

Tilly continued as Noah and Kelsie sat silently and respectfully listening. It was easy when they were walking along to forget how old Tilly was, but sitting listening to her like this, the life experience showed through the veneer of her physical youth. "Getting old is good in some ways. You learn not to worry so much. You learn to be thankful more, if you're smart. I've been kind of negative about marriage and it's sure got its ups and downs, but it's good to have someone to lay down with at night, to lean on during the days. Children are a sweet, heartbreaking blessing. They worry you like crazy, hurt you to the bone sometimes, but you would give anything and everything for them, because they're yours. Grandchildren are just that—grand. Fun to spoil, sweet to love on. Then they turn into teenagers and half of them run wild as bucks. It hurts to see them make the same mistakes your kids made, the same ones you made, but you it don't affect you quite as much because you know there is not one blessed thing you can do about it but pray and love. And sometimes fuss when you get a chance," she added with a chuckle.

"But the bad thing about age is that your memory goes, your strength goes, the arthritis hurts all the time, and doctors that look like school children poke you full of all the pills they can get your Medicare to pay for. Friends die, your companion dies, and you're alone a lot of the time.

47

Children get busy being parents and grandparents, and that's fine; that's the way it's supposed to be. But you miss them, still remember rocking a son that's some big strong man working down at the dock, with kids in college. You remember him in the still moments, and how small and smooth and worry free he once was, and when he comes by on Sunday afternoon, with the weight of the world on his shoulders and weariness in his eyes, you wish you could pick him up and rock him to sleep one more time." Tilly looked away, quickly. "Lord have mercy," she said. "I didn't need to go down that road."

Noah, sensing a need for a change in direction, asked Tilly, "Who do you want to see when we get to the city? Is there anyone special you want to look for?"

Tilly grinned at the question and the thought of the answer. "Why I want to see the Lord, first thing," she said quickly and definitely. "I'm gonna be looking for my husband Charles, and I've got a little girl over here that passed when she was two, but even they can wait a little while. These past few years, Jesus has been the only company I've had much of the time, and we've had a lot of conversations. He's been a good listener, but not much of a talker. So I want to see Him face to face."

"Did you see Him when you, uh, came through?" Kelsie inquired.

"No, honey, I did not," Tilly replied. "I just went to sleep and woke up lying in the grass on top of the mountain and knew right away where I was. That's just the way it happened. Why, did you see Him?" she asked looking from Kelsie to Noah, gauging their expressions.

Noah answered her question. "We saw Him at the accident site. He stood in a doorway and beckoned us over. But when we walked through, He wasn't there." Kelsie nodded and concurred with what Noah had said.

"Must be different for everybody," Tilly said. "I just came home in my sleep, so I didn't need no help. I just woke up here. But it was different for you. Didn't you say you waited for her?" she asked Noah, as he nodded. "That's probably why. The Good Lord gave you both a chance to come together. It must have been a part of His plan. As far as Him being on the mountain to greet us, I don't think it was necessary. It's pretty plain where we are and where we are going," she said, gesturing to the sparkling monolithic city wall rising out of the trees before them.

The group fell silent after that, pondering the journey before them and the thought of soon entering the most holy, fabled city in history. The Bible said little about it, but what it did was beyond comprehension. Now, they understood why. They had seen this land and from what they had seen of the city, it fit the descriptions. Over the years, many had tried to imagine its wonders and mysteries. Books, songs, poems, paintings and films had been devoted to the subject; all fell woefully short. The magnitude of sheer size, beauty and opulence, coupled with the deep clarity of perception they all experienced would have been sensory overload for the limits of human consciousness. It took a supernatural state of being to soak it all in.

While they sat upon the grass enjoying the surroundings, several animals came to the edge of the pool to drink. A small herd of reddish fallow deer, wandered down to the water and began to enjoy its cool refreshment. While they had seen butterflies, birds in flight, and an occasional squirrel in the trees, these were the first large animals they had seen. They had continued to see other people at a distance, and even exchanged friendly waves with a few, but none had come near; they were focused on traveling toward the city.

As the group watched the deer drinking from the pool, Noah spotted something in his peripheral vision to his immediate right. The sight shocked him, and he gestured to the others to be quiet and follow his gaze as he slowly turned his head. Two large panthers, tan in color, padded through the trees toward the pool. Their green eyes almost glowed with intensity, as the side of their smooth coats rippled with each stride. Although none of them had ever seen such large cats in the wild, they all noted that these panthers were shorter in length, stockier in build, and taller in height than any they had seen in books or on television. Kelsie exchanged anxious glances with Tilly and Noah. The outcome of this meeting might be tragic; if the panthers ran into the herd of deer, they might take one or more of the smaller ones. On the other hand, if the big cats spotted the three friends that were less than fifty yards to their left, Noah, Kelsie and Tilly had no idea what would happen.

Suddenly the silence was broken by Noah's voice. "Wait a second," he said, with no attempt at stealth or caution. "This is Heaven. We aren't going to get hurt, and chances are, they aren't going to attack those deer." The big cats had turned at the sound of his voice and stopped in their tracks, staring at him, while he stood and faced them.

"Are you sure about that?" Kelsie asked, slowly standing, and helping Tilly to her feet as well. They stood behind Noah as he assumed an almost confrontational stance, facing the pumas full on and meeting their gaze.

"Yes, I believe I am," Noah replied, with confidence building in his voice. "When God first made man, He gave us dominion over animals. Not only that, but there is no mention of death or any other predatory behavior in the Bible until after Adam and Eve sinned. I think when we got here, we got all that back," Noah stated. As if to prove the point, he extended an open hand toward the pair of mountain lions. "Come here, cats," Noah called to them, much like he would have called a pet. "Come to me. Come on."

The panthers looked at him for a moment, and began to pad toward him in docile submission. "Well, look at that," Tilly said. "Dr. Doolittle is talking to the animals."

The cats walked right up to Noah, and one touched his outstretched fingers with its wet nose, sniffing him for a moment before a rough pink tongue licked the palm of Noah's hand. The other rubbed against Noah's thigh like a huge house cat, nearly pushing him down with its display of affection. Noah ruffled the fur behind the first cat's ears with one hand and gingerly thumbed the panther's lip upward, exposing its teeth to satisfy his curiosity. "Check this out," Noah said to Kelsie. "Just as I expected. Look at these teeth."

The big cat's teeth were unlike any feline teeth Noah had ever seen. They were not sharp at all; no pointed incisors grew like fangs from the upper jaw. Instead, the teeth were broad, flat and even, like the teeth of a herbivore. Noah suspected that if he had looked at the teeth of the deer across the edge of the pool, he would have found their teeth remarkably similar. "They couldn't bite anything tougher than a biscuit," Noah declared.

Kelsie could see what he was talking about. "They aren't even made to eat meat. They must eat grass. That must be why they look so different."

Noah agreed. "Their whole body and digestive tract would be different as well. They're built more like a lamb than a lion," he quipped. "Which makes peaceful coexistence much more . . . peaceful."

Kelsie and Noah heard a startled and amused cry from behind them. "Hey," Tilly called, "A little help here, please." The other panther had rubbed past Noah and knocked Tilly down, purring and rubbing its head against her midsection like a giant tabby cat. Laughing, Tilly said, "Anybody got a saucer of milk? A ball of yarn? I think old Tom here needs something to play with besides me."

CHAPTER SEVEN

The two panthers laid at Noah's and Kelsie's feet, napping in the shade. Noah had named them Tom and Tonya, and the surprisingly docile creatures had been lulled to sleep by the sound of the rushing waters of the spring. While none of their group had felt sleepy or tired, they knew that sleep was instinctive behavior for cats, both large and small, so it had not surprised them to see several hundred pounds of feline flesh stretched out on the grass, purring in peaceful slumber.

Noah, Kelsie and Tilly drank their fill of the cold clear water from the pool, before Tilly announced that she was going to take a walk and see what kind of fruit and nuts might be readily available. She promised to be back soon, but none of them seemed to be in a big hurry to leave this place. The spring was beautiful, and the city would be waiting when they got there.

As they laid side by side in the grass, staring through the canopy of leaves above, Kelsie thought about what Tilly had said about their relationship. "Tilly was right, wasn't she?" Kelsie asked. "Things are different now for us. I mean, I love you more than ever, but it's different." She struggled with how to put it into words without being blatant.

Noah had no such reservations. "You mean it's not physical. There's no sexual enticement, right? I'd have to say she's right. I love you too. I mean deeply and sincerely, knowing what that really means more than I ever did before. But the arousal of sexual desire is just . . . gone. Not like I lost it, just like it's not supposed to be there."

Kelsie turned to him, propping herself up on one elbow. "Does that bother you?" she asked. "Because I gotta say, it doesn't bother me. I thought it would. But it just makes life easier. Does that make sense?"

Noah turned his head and looked into her big blue eyes. "Strangely enough, it almost feels like a relief. I've got to admit, Kelsie, that I'm a guy. When we started dating, I didn't want to go too fast, to mess up. I wanted to *respect* you. I wanted to wait, but it made me crazy sometimes. I wanted to be with you physically so bad, it almost literally hurt. But now, the whole carnal nature is just 'poof'- it's gone. And I don't miss it. Not at all. If anybody had told me that, I would have said they were crazy. But I'm happy . . . completely happy." He smiled a very satisfied smile.

"Me too," Kelsie agreed. "And it makes the jealousy thing in a relationship not really matter either. I mean, I know you still love Kayla. You practically told me as much. You still felt a responsibility toward her. That made me a little jealous."

"A little?" Noah smirked.

"Okay, it made me a lot jealous. You had a history. But now, none of it seems to matter."

"You really mean that, don't you?" Noah asked.

"Of course I do," Kelsie replied. "There is never going to be a competition for your love and attention anymore. There just isn't. Love here isn't sexual, but it isn't *exclusive* either. I was always taught, 'You're supposed to love everybody'. Well, that's never been truer than here. It's natural and it's okay."

"I cannot tell you how much easier my life is because of that," Noah replied. "I did love Kayla. I still do. I was protective of her, and that little green eyed firecracker still made me crazy. It was complicated, but I wanted so badly to be good to her and take care of her, even though I loved you. I wanted to at least be her friend, but when you've been as close as we were…" he trailed off. "It's just hard. She thought I was going to always be there. We had talked about a future together. It was stormy sometimes, but what relationship isn't? Her mother got mad at me, but I think she was just hurt and disappointed. She had high expectations of my relationship with Kayla too. I guess we all did, but it just didn't work out that way. Of course, that's not the only complication you and I had in life. I know you cared about Tyler too. It really wasn't fair the way I swooped in and stole you away."

"The last time I checked, you didn't exactly tie me up and 'steal' me," Kelsie said. "Tyler is sweet and he's a good friend, and I love him like a friend. But you and I were drawn together. Okay, so maybe you were a charmer, but I think there was more to it than that. Heck, I'm smarter than that. I didn't fall for you because you were Mr. Smooth. I couldn't get you out of my head. Now I think I know why. We thought we would spend the rest of our life together, because we *did* spend the rest of our life together. We were supposed to die together. We were supposed to come here together. It was meant to be."

"This must be Heaven," Noah said. "We just discussed some of the most complicated issues in our relationship like it was no big deal. Nobody could talk about that stuff on the other side without a complete meltdown," he mused. "Life is so messed up. I'm glad it's over."

"Oh I don't think it's over," Kelsie countered. "I just think it's changed. Just because we've left all that baggage behind doesn't mean we can lie here on the grass with the cats forever. We've got to go to the city. There are things to do. There are reasons we're here. Heaven's not an eternal vacation."

"Are you sure we didn't get married somewhere along the way? Because you are beginning to sound like a wife," Noah teased. "Seriously, I agree. When Tilly gets back, we'll get going. I know we've got eternity, but I still don't like to waste time. Even over there, I only slept when I just had to. I want to see Jesus as badly as Tilly. I want to see more of this place. And I'm like you- I've got a feeling God's got work for us to do."

Kelsie processed their deep discussion, while idly staring at the huge mountain lions lying at their feet. It was a surreal moment. "So do you think we own a couple of cats, now?"

Noah shrugged. "I'm not sure that anybody ever owns a cat. They just choose whom they want to hang out with."

Kelsie smiled. "I'm glad that they picked us."

Noah looked at her, and hugged her, holding her tightly. "I'm glad that you picked me," he said. Kelsie kissed him lightly, gently and innocently. It felt wonderful.

"So I'm gone for . . . well, I don't know how long I was gone, but it seems like no time, and here you are all hugged up. Ya'll need a moment?" Tilly asked, as she came walking into the clearing with a large patch of berries gathered in the skirt of her cotton dress.

"No, we're good," Kelsie replied smiling, getting on her feet. "So what did you find? Looks like big blackberries."

"Honey, these don't taste like blackberries," Tilly said with a grin. "They taste like blackberry *cobbler*. Sugar, butter, even a hint of cinnamon. It's all in there."

Noah reached for one and popped it in his mouth. The sweet juice poured down his throat; slightly warm, like a pie set on a window ledge to cool. "Oh wow! That is incredible! You got any ice cream?" he joked.

"Not yet, but if it grows on a bush around here, I aim to find it," Tilly replied.

CHAPTER EIGHT

To say that it was late in the day when the group continued on the way to the city made no sense to any of them, since there was no night, no morning, no evening and no perception of hours passing. But late in the day was what it felt like, using the beginning of their descent down the mountains as a point of reference. Upon discussing the idea, Noah said that he considered the point of entry on the mountain top to be like morning, and thought that the reason they perceived the time to be late in the afternoon, was because of the rest stop they made at the spring, after a substantial amount of progress.

Kelsie thought it was because they were under the shade of the trees, giving it a late afternoon feel. Tilly had a totally different idea; her theory was centered around the meal of cobbler berries and pecans they had eaten. To her, it felt like a late lunch, making it seem like later in the afternoon. Thus the trio all had different reasons for perceiving the time of day, but they all agreed on the general context of time.

As the trio continued however, the absence of dusk caused the perception to wane. They traveled for what seemed like many miles through the thick canopy of trees, with the pair of large mountain lions walking by their side. No night approached; no moon or stars appeared. They continued to discover a number of new flowers, shrubs and trees, including a large bush that produced fruits with a rind like citrus, but with the flavor and texture of beef. Noah was amazed and insisted on carrying a couple of fruits with him, just in case these bushes were rare.

As they continued on their way, the trees began to thin and large clearings became more prevalent. Fellow travelers seemed more plentiful. While passing through one of these fields, Kelsie struck up a conversation with a man from North Korea named Jin Gi. The man was fascinated with Kelsie's appearance because he couldn't remember ever seeing a woman with natural red hair. "I have lived a very closed existence in my country," Jin Gi said, with a distant look in his eyes.

Jin Gi shared with the group that he had died in a prison camp because of his Christian faith. Although his appearance was as perfect as the rest, the man said he had been imprisoned and tortured for several years before his body finally gave out due to an extended bout of untreated pneumonia. He told the group he felt as if he had gained thirty pounds as soon as he woke up here. "I cannot wait to see *Jesu Nim*!" he exclaimed. "I will see you again in the city," Jin Gi said before hurrying along ahead of them.

Noah watched the man as he dropped into an easy runner's pace and faded out of view. "Did you notice anything different about that conversation?" he asked, looking at Kelsie.

"Just that he spoke Korean when he referred to Jesus," Kelsie replied.

Tilly looked at Noah, knowing what he was thinking. "Honey," she said, "He spoke Korean the whole time. He spoke Korean and you spoke English and ya'll just understood each other. You both had the gift of interpretation at the same time."

"What about you two?" Kelsie asked. "Could you both understand him?"

"Yeah, we did, but I think we were more aware that he was speaking Korean," Noah replied, as Tilly nodded in agreement. "I think because you were both talking to each other, you didn't even notice."

"Pretty cool, huh?" Kelsie replied. "Bet you didn't know I could understand Korean."

"What's even more amazing is that you could probably *speak* Korean, if you tried," Tilly stated. "You almost seemed like you were about to, at one point. I think we know what we need to know, when we need to know it. We don't just have perfected bodies . . . we have perfected *minds*," Tilly said, tapping her temple with her index finger.

Noah thought about that for a moment. "If that's the case, I wonder if we could just skip talking and read each other's minds?"

Kelsie laughed. "I doubt it. That seems more like something out of Hell than Heaven. Can you imagine everyone knowing what you were thinking and knowing what everybody else is thinking? I've got friends that would strangle one another if they could read minds."

Tilly smirked at that. "Not as bad here as it would be on the other side, when we still had the carnal nature. There is no malice, no selfishness, no real need for secrets anymore. Still, I think you're right. We would feel like our privacy is invaded. I don't think God would do that."

As the trio neared the city, they began to see signs of development. Houses, with manicured grounds, dotted the countryside. Some appeared to have been built for a long time, while a few of the homes they saw were still under construction. While most of the houses were fairly large, and quite beautiful, none seemed to fit the traditional idea of sparkling mansions that the group had grown up with. The homes displayed a variety of styles from a myriad of cultures, plus styles unknown to any culture except Heaven. Each home had plenty of room, without the selfish waste and decadence that came with the need to impress others that permeated much of the other side. Still, the design and craftsmanship of these homes was impressive on a grand scale, and Noah's experience in the building trades made several things apparent about the construction methods almost immediately.

First, there were no fasteners. No nails, screws, pegs, or even glue was visible. These houses seemed to just stay together of their own accord. While a good deal of intricate woodwork was visible on many buildings, no notches or joints were used to hold any of the framing or finish work together.

Secondly, Noah had never seen finishes so smooth, straight and perfect. Every piece of siding, every framing member, every window and every door were so perfectly fit that a human hair would not fit between them. He had never seen work so perfect, finishes so well done.

Finally, the materials, designs, and angles used in many of these buildings seemed to defy the laws of physics. Noah noticed an Asian themed home, with delicate paper paneled walls and thin black lacquered framing, supporting a roof made of solid red granite slabs that must have weighed many tons. The group waved to a resident of a low sprawling ranch. He was sitting on his back porch that hung perhaps sixty feet over the bank of a large stream, with no visible means of support. It was as if the laws of nature had been suspended or permanently revoked.

Submission, thought Noah. *The makeup of Heaven submits to us. The plants, the animals, the stone, even gravity and kinetic energy bend to our will. Incredible,* he thought to himself.

"Wonder why there are so many houses outside the city?" Tilly thought aloud.

"Yeah I was wondering the same thing," Kelsie replied. "I figured all the mansions would be inside the city."

"Do you want to live in a city?" Noah asked, looking at either of them. They both shook their heads in the negative. "Me either," Noah replied. "I got a feeling that the city has room for those that like city life and plenty of room outside for those that don't. I've heard my dad talk about some denominations that claimed their church was 'The Bride' and that members of that church live in the city, while Christians that weren't a part of that church live outside, but he didn't put a lot of stock in that. I don't guess I never thought much about it. If I get a chance to choose, I like the idea of living out here just fine."

Regardless of their desires for living space, the three all agreed; they wanted to see the city. More specifically, they wanted to see Jesus, who dwelt in the city. They wanted to see friends, family and people from history and the Bible. They were drawing ever nearer; the top of the walls could no longer be seen.

As they came to the top of a low grassy hill and stopped for a moment to let the big cats graze, they saw the path that would lead them to their destination. As they gazed on a broad, sparkling highway below them with a steady stream of people walking in the same direction, it was apparent that they would soon be there.

CHAPTER NINE

T he road on which they traveled was one of twelve broad, straight highways, each leading to a gate of the city. As foretold by the apostle John, the highway was paved with gold, so pure, that it seemed almost transparent. Its detail, however, was much more in depth than the trio of travelers could have imagined.

The highway was curbed with large oblong pieces of semi-precious stones, over four feet in length and a foot wide. Jade, amethyst, agate, lapis lazuli, turquoise, and others were placed end to end along the edge, in a ribbon of color and brilliance. Benches were cut from solid boulders of pink, blue, and clear quartz and placed beside the road at regular intervals. Cut crystal fountains full of cool, clear, bubbling water were used on both sides of the highway as mile markers.

The pavement was comprised of large gold bricks, each one inscribed ornately with Biblical scripture. Each scripture was related in some way to a righteous journey. Kelsie read one aloud. "You make known to me the path of life; in your presence there is fullness of joy; at your right hand are pleasures forevermore. – Psalms 16:11 (ESV)."

Tilly bent and read another. "Because strait [is] the gate, and narrow [is] the way, which leadeth unto life, and few there be that find it. – Matthew 7:14 (KJV)." Tilly smiled. "We're doing it again. These are written in Hebrew, but we're reading them in English."

"Maybe we just think we're reading them in English," Noah replied. "Maybe we are all speaking Hebrew. Or maybe it doesn't matter. Anyway, it's pretty cool." He glanced over at Kelsie, who was standing still, looking back up the hill at the way they had come. "What's the matter?" he asked.

"I think we've lost our escorts," Kelsie said, pointing at the mountain lions that had traveled with them for many miles. "Tom and Tonya don't seem to want to take the highway." The big cats stared back at their traveling companions from the top of the hill

"Bummer," said Noah. "I guess it's just as well. They've come a long way with us. They will probably go back to where they came from."

Tilly waved and called to them. "Goodbye, my big ole' kitty cats. Never was much of a cat person, but you two have grown on me."

"Yeah, I hear ya," Noah said. "But I guess they have their place and we have ours. Speaking of which . . . shall we head out? I'm feeling like Dorothy on the Yellow Brick Road. Almost want to break into a skip."

"Well, you're looking more like the Scarecrow," Kelsie shot back with a laugh and a wink. "Come on. Let's go."

The group walked along at a crisp pace, kept in part by the flow of foot traffic around them. Hundreds of people surrounded them, but there was plenty of room. The roadway was broad, perhaps a hundred yards in width. The threesome chatted with others as they went.

The people they talked with were from all walks of life, from many different nations, and many different races. Tilly talked to a Russian woman named Greta, while Kelsie listened as a fisherman from Patagonia spoke of catching sea bass off the coast of Chile, where he had suddenly fell overboard. "One minute, I was pulling in the nets, the next, I was standing on a mountaintop," he said, his big dark eyes sparkling at the thought.

Most of the people they talked to had passed into Heaven as a result of natural causes. Many of the ones they spoke with were like Tilly. They had lived long lives, and went from being old and feeble to young and vibrant again. They were all excited; all enjoyed the newfound youth, strength and perfection. Some had related similar stories to Tilly's. Where they had carried a scar in life that signified a life changing event, they carried a small benign reminder. The scars were painless and hardly noticeable, but they were there as a memorial to the sacrifice their body had made in life.

"I wonder why we don't carry any scars," Noah said, looking at Kelsie. "We went through a rough wreck. I was . . . I was really broken up," he said finally, after a long pause. "I'm glad you didn't have to see me that way. But you would think we would carry some reminder."

Kelsie took his hand. "I don't think we have any scars because we didn't live to carry any scars. We went straight from there to here. And I did see myself, briefly. I don't know about you, but I don't want any reminders."

"Me either," Noah replied, giving her hand a squeeze. Kelsie was right, he thought to himself. They didn't need any reminders, and thankfully, the accident was already fading from memory, like a dream.

They continued to be amazed at the variety and peaceful exuberance of the people. They were all moving together, all full of energy and love, all full of excitement and anticipation. What surprised the group the most though, were the children.

Throughout the crowd, there were several children of various ages. Some traveled with others; some seemed to be alone.

Noah talked with a beautiful fair haired little girl named Jessica that said she was seven. "Leukemia," was the answer she had given him, when he had asked her how she got there. "Jesus took my hand and led me right out of my room. Momma and Daddy were crying, but He said they would see me again, so I didn't feel so bad. He gave me my hair back!" she exclaimed, touching her thick blond locks. "He carried me down from the mountain and told me to follow the other people. He said I would be fine."

"Wow," Noah said. "Just . . . wow. I've got to ask you something. Did Jesus say anything about you being a kid? I mean, we've seen old people that became young, but I haven't thought about the 'being a kid' part." He looked around, noticing more than a few children of various ages. One little boy that couldn't have been more than five was holding the hand of a woman that may or may not have been his mother.

"He said I get to pick," the little girl replied. "If I want to grow up, I can, but I don't have to. He said I would never get old, but if I got tired of being a little girl, I would just naturally grow up a little at a time. Neat, huh?"

"Neat, indeed," Noah replied with a grin. He thought about how when he was four, he never wanted to get older. He enjoyed being four. He enjoyed staying at his Mamaw's house, watching cartoons, playing in the back yard, drinking chocolate milk and not having a care in the world. For these kids, they could have eternal childhood, if they chose. But one thing still bothered him. "Who is going to take care of you?"

The little girl smiled a knowing smile. "I can take of myself. I may be a kid, but I'm as smart as you. In fact, I'm smarter than my parents, the doctors, or anybody else on the other side."

Noah recalled Tilly's words. *We don't just have perfected bodies . . . we have perfected minds.* He understood how these kids would get along in Heaven. No dangers existed and food literally grew on trees in abundance. They would function just as well and probably better than adults. Children have much better imaginations and little consideration to physical limitations. They could jump into a world like this and feel right at home. *If I could find a chocolate milk fountain around here, I'd sign up for that deal myself,* Noah thought to himself with a grin.

Jessica walked with Noah, Kelsie and Tilly during the trip toward the city. They stopped at one of the fountains for a drink and ventured off the highway to pick a few ripe bananas from a nearby grove. Noah broke out the one of the bush-beef fruits he had been carrying and offered it to share with his companions, but there were no takers. "You know, I've seen those things growing everywhere the past few miles," Kelsie remarked. "You don't have to keep carrying them with you."

"I know," Noah replied, "But it's got warm in my pocket. Almost tastes like it just came off the grill." He held it out to Jessica.

The little girl shook her head. "I ate a *dvash* about an hour ago," Jessica said. "I don't know if I would like those anyway. I haven't had much of an appetite for a while. I feel great . . . it just takes getting used to." She made a little face.

"I hear you, baby," Tilly said, putting her arm around her. "It's taking me a while to get used to having teeth again!" she added with a little snort. Tilly was obviously pleased with Jessica choosing to travel with them. She seemed immediately enamored with the girl, her maternal instincts kicking in. Jessica snuggled a little closer into the crook of Tilly's arm, pleased with the attention.

The group continued on their journey down the highway as it led into a wooded area with oaks so tall and broad, they obstructed the view of the city for a time. During this stint of the trip, they met a couple from North Dakota who had been married for fifty seven years and passed when Edgar, the gentleman of the pair, had fallen asleep at the wheel of their 1988 Crown Victoria and struck a bridge abutment. They had experienced a similar passage to Noah and Kelsie; only Christine said she had waited for Edgar for a few moments, before they had both followed the familiar figure of Jesus through a doorway into this world.

When they stepped out onto Heaven's side, Edgar said he almost didn't recognize Christine for a moment, until he remembered her for the stunning beauty she had been so many years before. She was an incredibly beautiful woman, with large hazel eyes, porcelain skin and full red lips. She was also seventy seven years old, although now, she appeared to be perhaps twenty five. Edgar's youth appearance was also striking. He was tall and broad shouldered, perhaps two hundred pounds, with a solid jaw and a thick shock of raven hair, parted to one side. He was eighty, but looked like a movie star from the 1950's, which ironically seemed appropriate, since he had auditioned unsuccessfully for the role of Tarzan in 1952.

He had traveled to Hollywood to become a star. The only bright spot he had found in the California sun, was a nineteen year old waitress named Christine. He had taken her back to North Dakota and they, in time, had taken over the family farm. "I wasn't always good to her," Edgar said, taking her hand, "But she was always there for me. She's worked harder than most men, and raised four good kids. Now she's got her reward."

"Looks like you've got yours too," Kelsie said, smiling at the sweet couple. "You got Heaven, plus an angel to keep you company."

Christine gave Kelsie a wry smile. "I appreciate the compliment, sweetie, but obviously, you haven't seen an angel yet."

Kelsie's eyes widened with wonder. None of them had even thought about it. "Have you?" she asked, looking at the couple in astonishment.

"Oh yeah, that we have," Christine replied. "Apparently there was one stationed as a guard or sentinel or something on the mountain, not far from where we came through. He just nodded to us, welcomed us and gestured for us to proceed down the mountain."

"What did he look like?" Tilly asked, obviously caught up in the curiosity.

"Big, buff, and bad," Edgar said. "He was tall enough to play for the Lakers and looked like he could take on a squad of Special Forces. This was not your momma's little glass figurine. No wings, no harp, no fat little cherub. Just a very big guy in a simple white robe, with a big ole' sword strapped to his hip. Nice enough, though. He said 'Welcome, son and daughter of man. You have reached your home land. You may proceed to the city at your convenience.' Then he just returned to his post."

"I wonder why they would have a guard?" Kelsie thought aloud. "Surely God isn't expecting an attack on Heaven."

"Not anymore," Noah said. "There was a battle here, a long time ago, when Satan and the demons were cast out. Now, I would say that the guards are just a symbol. They are probably there to help travelers more than anything. Plus, they make you feel safe."

"Like a guardian angel," Jessica said, with a sudden revelation.

Tilly put her arm around her and gave her a loving pat. "Why yes baby, I would say that's kind of what they are; except they are guardian angels for here, instead of there."

Edgar and Christine joined Noah, Kelsie, Tilly and Jessica, as the group continued toward the city. They talked of their past lives; they talked about what they hoped to find. They greeted fellow travelers. Jessica met a boy from Spain about her age and they shared stories about school and friends that were already behind them. But the thing that was on all of their minds was the future that lay ahead.

CHAPTER TEN

When the group drew within five miles of the city, they saw the honor guard of angels posted on each side of the road at regular intervals, armed with a long two edged sword at their side, a spear in one hand and an ornate shield in the other. They were, as Edgar and Christine described, very large and powerful looking; most of them were at least seven feet tall. They were all male in appearance. While they were dressed in identical robes, the angels were as unique in features as humans. Some had the appearance of various human races, while others appeared to be from a race unknown anywhere on Earth.

Even though the honor guard stood at attention, they were friendly, and would engage in conversation when approached. One fierce looking warrior angel, with the broad dark features of an Aborigine smiled at Jessica as she passed, and said, "Welcome, little one! Your home and your Father awaits!" Jessica responded with a bashful smile as she slowly walked by.

Noah approached another angel with shoulder length blonde hair and a short beard. He shot the angel a conspiratorial smile and casually commented, "You guys seem pretty pumped, for such a boring detail."

"A boring detail?" the angel responded. "On the contrary, a post with the honor guard is highly regarded. The angelic armies take these posts in rotation. Many of us have spent considerable time on the other side. We enjoy watching the sons and daughters of man come home. Occasionally, we are even fortunate enough to see someone we've helped in the past. It is almost like seeing an old friend."

"Does anyone ever recognize you?" Kelsie asked. "Do they remember having seen you on the other side?"

The angel shook his head. "Almost never. We normally don't appear in material form. Many of the times when we have, it has been to deal with individuals that rarely wind up here," he said with a grim smile, as tactfully as he could manage.

"How many of you are stationed on the honor guard?" Edgar asked. He was looking down the highway at the row of angels on either side.

"A legion assigned to each gate. That is six thousand. Seventy two thousand total, not counting the pairs of cherubim at each gate," the angel answered.

"Cherubim," repeated Noah, the wheels turning in his mind. "Why only two at each gate, when there are ten of thousands of you?"

The angel looked at him intently. "Cherubim are very rare. There are not very many of them. Most of them are assigned to very specialized tasks."

"Kind of like an endangered species, huh?" Jessica countered.

The angel laughed out loud. "You are funny, little one. You make a joke, right? Cherubim aren't endangered by anything or anyone. They are a force of creation that has no equal."

"I remember reading about them in Ezekiel," Tilly said. "They are made different. Are they like a man, or like an animal?"

"Both," the angel said, " . . . and neither. They are a hybrid, a very powerful being, as you will soon see for yourselves."

The group continued on. The excitement was so thick among the crowds, it was almost palatable. While the people were orderly, their voices seemed to crash against the city walls and reverberate, like ocean waves against a mighty mountain.

As they drew near, they could see the city's foundations, laid to support the immense walls that stretched into the sky farther than the eye could see. The walls towered so far, it seemed as if the foundations would need to be many miles high and just as thick. Since the physical laws of gravity did not necessarily apply, however, the top of the foundations were in sight of the ground.

The city's foundations extended at least about a hundred yards in height from the base, comprised of 12 layers of semiprecious stone. At the bottom was the same jasper crystal that comprised the walls of the city. Inscribed into every huge stone of it was the name *SIMON PETER BARJONAH* in bold letters, three feet high, inlaid with gold. The next layer was made of cobalt blue slabs of sapphire, inscribed in the same manner with the name *ANDREW BARJONAH.* The following layer was made of an amber quartz called chalcedony, inscribed with the name *JAMES BOANERGES;* the next was of brilliant green emerald, upon which was written *JOHN BOANERGES – He whom Jesus loves.*

The fifth layer of foundation was made of sardonyx, a red striped onyx stone, with the name *PHILIP* emblazoned across every stone. The sixth was deep orange sardius, wearing the name of *THOMAS DIDYMUS;* the seventh was a transparent greenish gold stone called chrysolite with the name *BARTHOLOMEW.* The eighth was made of aquamarine colored beryl, with the name *MATTHEW LEVI;* the ninth was pink topaz, with the name *JAMES OF ALPHAEUS* cut into it. The tenth foundation was made of a pale green stone called chrysorasus, inscribed with *SIMON ZELOTES* and the eleventh section was made of transparent red jacinth, imprinted with the name of *THADDAEUS - also known as JUDAS BARJAMES.*

The top layer of foundation was made of purple amethyst, and the inscription was *MATHIAS*. From there, the walls extended skyward. The end effect made the city look as if it rested upon a massive stone rainbow. It was beautiful and elegant, with a look that was truly indescribable. The foundation was completely visible, with the exception of a long wide ramp of transparent gold that led to the gate the group was approaching.

The gate opening loomed cavernously above their heads; its area consisted of an arch large enough to fly two airliners through, wingtip to wingtip. Gates made of enormous singular fresh water pearls were hung on hinge pins eight feet thick. The gates had no bolt or latch. Since the land of Heaven was completely secure, they had never been closed and would never be closed.

On either side of the gate sat the cherubim. They stood slightly more than ten feet tall, and despite the friendly attitude displayed by the angelic honor guard, there was something incredibly fierce and dangerous about their look. Where the angels they had seen were basically human in appearance, the cherubim were obviously not like anything on the other side.

Each cherubim had four heads which grew from a very broad set of muscular shoulders. While one head was humanoid, with thick dark curly hair, the one beside it looked like a lion, with a short thick muzzle and the tips of long sharp teeth peeking out from beneath its jowls. The head to its immediate left was that of an ox, with an impressive set of horns that grew out of a thatch of curls that matched the hair of the humanoid head. The last head looked like a fierce gigantic eagle, with a hooked beak and piercing eyes.

From the backs of the cherubim grew four wings, covered with deep auburn feathers. Where each wing grew from a cherub's back, a matching arm grew from its thick midsection. Each cherub stood on legs like tree trunks, which ended with huge black cloven hooves.

As the group of travelers approached, eight sets of intense, intelligent eyes passed over them carefully, in solemn vigilance. A couple of the cherubim's heads nodded in acknowledgement, while the rest of the faces swept the throng of people coming down the road.

While the cherubim, the honor guard and the city walls provided a show of force and fortification unlike anything the world had ever seen, Noah realized that it was all merely for the pleasure and the glory of God. This land needed no walled cities with massive gates, no angelic armies, and no fierce cherubs to stand watch. This was all a display of God's might and authority.

Kelsie squeezed Noah's hand tightly, as Jessica did the same to Tilly. Edgar walked with his arm resting around Christine's shoulder. "This is it, isn't it?" Kelsie said looking into Noah's eyes. This really is the place. This is Heaven, just like Sunday School and night time prayers. Nothing will ever be the same."

Noah kissed her lightly on the cheek and said, "Kelsie, nothing was ever the same from the time I got saved when I was five years old. Nothing was ever the same after I met a tall red headed country girl with a flavor for camo and cowboy boots. Nothing was definitely the same after I rode that stretch of College Street on the way back home from your house. Now, everything until this moment is going to feel like a dream in comparison. We are about to realize our entire potential. Let's go meet our Maker."

CHAPTER ELEVEN

This was New Jerusalem, the capital city of Heaven, the home of Jehovah God, the Father and Creator of everything. It had taken its name from the city that was once called simply Salem, which means *peace*. Sometime later, during the four hundred and fifty year period between Abraham's visit with the priest king Melchizedek and the period when Joshua led the Israelites in the taking of Canaan, the name of the city was changed to Jerusalem, which means *the teaching of peace*. This was extremely ironic, because even though God ordained Jerusalem as the holy city where His earthy temple would be built, it was one of the least peaceful places on Earth. Jerusalem in Israel had been at war and under siege from the outside and the inside for thousands of years.

Like many other cities that have taken their names from other places, New Jerusalem did not resemble its namesake at all.

The city had been built fairly recently, by eternal standards. When Jesus said, "I go to prepare a place before you", He meant that quite literally. Before He came, those that had 'passed on' went to a place the Hebrews called Sheol. It was the place of the dead. There, the land was divided by a huge chasm into Paradise, sometimes referred to as Abraham's Bosom, and Gehenna, also known as Hell or the Pit.

During the three days that Jesus' body had been in the tomb, He had traveled to Sheol for those righteous dead that had followed Jehovah. Jesus took them from Paradise to the land of Heaven, where they founded and began to help build New Jerusalem. With Paradise empty, a huge quake had overtaken the unoccupied territory, and the land collapsed into the chasm, becoming part of Gehenna.

New Jerusalem, as the travelers could easily see, was the *real* city of "peace". Every street was lined by trees, flowers, and people, full of life and full of peace. Songbirds the size of butterflies and butterflies the size of songbirds flitted about, sharing their beauty and song with the masses. Squirrels with full, bushy tails and even a few small, bright colored monkeys played in the branches of the trees. Street vendors were parked on the sidewalks giving, not selling their wares to passersby, and several musicians could be seen on street corners, lending their virtuoso talents to the ambience of the cityscape.

As the group walked through the gateway into the city, they, like others slowed to a stroll, taking it all in. As Kelsie and Jessica both stood with childlike wonder, eyes wide and mouths open, Edgar and Christine beamed at each other. "I'm so happy I could cry, if I could cry anymore," Christine said. "I don't even know what to say or do."

"Well I do!" Tilly said, and broke into a full sprint down the street, shouting and jumping, with the fervency that she had seen in her mother during summer revivals at her home church as a child. "WOOOHOOOO! PRAISE JESUS! THANK YOU LORD! OH GOD, THANKS BE UNTO YOU WHO WAS AND IS AND IS TO COME!" Tilly shouted at the top of her lungs, running to the nearest street corner, and returning, making a lap around her friends before finally settled down. "Ya'll watch out. I think I may have another spell of that on the way," she said, laughing.

Tilly wasn't the only one that had that kind of reaction. As the stream of people came through the gate, several shouted and ran down the street, their voice full of praise and joy. More than one just kept running until they were out of sight.

Noah just stood there with a broad grin across his face. He said nothing, but just watched his friends as they soaked in the marvels of their surroundings. The people, the beautiful buildings and the life pulse of the city was amazing. Noah paused for a moment as something in the background was tugging at his attention. As he listened, he could hear a nearby guitarist playing a familiar riff and singing:

Don't look back
A new day is breakin'
It's been too long since I felt this way
I don't mind where I get taken

The road is callin'
Today is the day

I can see
It took so long just to realize
I'm much too strong
Not to compromise
Now I see what I am is holding me down
I'll turn it around, oh yes I will...

"Boston," Noah said, turning to Kelsie. "Very cool . . . and very appropriate, although I never knew why I liked that song until now."

Kelsie laughed and said, "Well don't expect to every song on your old play list around here. Some of that stuff is better left on the other side."

"Don't worry," Noah replied. "I'm sure there is plenty of new stuff to listen to here. I might even get to write a little."

"I'm sure if you want, you'll get to write a lot," Edgar interjected. "From what I can see, these folks are staying busy, but they are staying busy with things they enjoy doing."

Christine smiled at that. "Ed! I have always wanted to paint! You know I've mentioned it over the years, but by the time the kids were grown, I figured it was too late."

"It's not too late for anything anymore," Edgar replied. "You've got all the time you need."

"Time to play," Jessica said, wistfully.

"Yes, time to play. That actually sounds pretty good," Kelsie agreed.

"Time to talk, to visit, to love," Tilly said. "No hurries and no worries."

"What do we do first?" asked Christine.

"Not meaning to cut to the chase," said Noah, "But I think the first thing we do is go see Jesus."

The group agreed. Before heading into the city, however, they stopped at a nearby food stand, serving the most incredible gyros and fresh fried chips that any of them had ever tasted. Edgar asked the proprietor, a Serbian man with a thick mustache and olive skin, how long he had been doing this. "I'm not really sure," he said with a smile. "Time slips away here. I can tell you that I came over in July of 1991. I had been conscripted in the army, but was trying to get away from a conflict in the middle of Yugoslavia when I got caught in a shell attack. One minute I was running down a street; the next I was here."

Edgar nodded. "I think that was the conflict they call the Ten Day War. It's been nearly twenty years ago."

"Nearly twenty years," the Serbian replied thoughtfully. "Seems like last week. Not that I'm complaining. Time has no meaning here. Minutes, days, decades or centuries; they are all anachronisms in Heaven."

Tilly pressed the man with a question. "I've got to ask. This is Heaven. You could do anything you want. Why are you running a street food stand?"

"Because God likes really good gyros," he said with a twinkle in his eye. "Actually, I love to cook and love to serve people. This is Heaven to me. I will do this until I get tired of it, then maybe I will do something else. But right now, I'm loving it," he continued before adding, " . . . and it's as far from being a soldier as I can get."

Edgar asked food vendor about the direction they needed to go to get to the throne. "Actually, it's The Thrones," he replied. "There is more than one, you know. The street you stand on, Reuben Way, leads to The Thrones. Each street that comes from a city gate is named after one of the twelve tribes of Israel. They all converge at The Thrones. As they say, 'You can't miss it.' Just follow the people and the light coming from the city square."

"Just go into the light, huh?" Noah said with a chuckle. His friends just stared at him blankly. "Oh come on! You know, 'the light'? Like when you're dead. I know you got that."

"Oh we got it all right," said Kelsie. "You just didn't get a perfect sense of humor to go with the perfect everything else," she said with a wink.

As the group of friends proceeded down Reuben Way, they listened to musicians improvise amazing riffs that seemed physically impossible. They watched as, to Jessica's delight, an artist painted a stunning three dimensional portrait of her in great detail. It looked as if you could reach into the canvas.

Noah thought about the possibilities of having the time to do what he wanted. What did he want to do? He loved to play music. He could learn every instrument known to man, and probably several that weren't. He could pursue his love for art, drawing or painting in vivid color and detail that he couldn't imagine before. He might try his hand at building, working in wood or stone or metal. The thing was, he could probably do all of these. After all, he had all the time he would ever need. That was one of the most incredible things about this place.

He looked at the buildings around them. Some were vast; some were fairly small, but quite ornate and interesting. The designs were as varied and challenging to the laws of physics as any they had seen in the countryside; perhaps more so. Something about their design and variety reminded him of a book he had read as a child. It was called "Oh The Places You'll Go!" by Dr. Suess, and it was full of illustrations of fantastic lands, creatures and structures. While New Jerusalem lacked the cartoonish quality of the book, its locales, life and architecture were more varied and fantastic than anything the creative mind of a bestselling children's author could have imagined. *Oh, the places you'll go indeed,* Noah thought to himself.

Christine and Kelsie were fast becoming good friends. Even though their life experiences were six decades apart, they shared the same fun loving zeal for life. Christine had always retained a shadow of the vivacious nature she once had when she was young; now, it was coming back into full force as she enjoyed the vibrancy of her new life.

"So this guy," Christine said, gesturing to Noah, who was walking ahead of them talking to Edgar about the magnificent architecture of some of the buildings, "He must have been something special to you on the other side. Is he your boyfriend?"

Kelsie smiled and blushed a bit. "You know, that's a complicated question now. He was, and I'm still crazy about him, you know? He is the most charming, giving, loving guy I ever met. When he was trying to get me to go out with him, he bought me a set of amazing diamond earrings. Not as a bribe, but as a gesture, you know? He didn't make a lot of money, but he just loved to give. He said, 'You may never date me, but I never want you to forget me.' I was hooked. We had talked about a life together, and now things are good, but they are different. It's still love, but it's a different kind of love. Do you know what I mean?"

Christine returned her smile and nodded. "I know just what you mean. Edgar and I have been together for most of our lives. It wasn't always fun, but it was always good. We had a pretty good talk on the way down to the city before you saw us. At the age we were, there wasn't a lot of physical stuff anymore. But we were closer than ever. Best friends, that's what we were, and still are. For us, things haven't changed that much, other than feeling better than we ever did. We've decided we want to stay close. I don't know if that's possible, but if it is, we'll make it work. It's not like marriage anymore, but that doesn't mean it's not a good thing. We may take a little while to pursue our own interests. I mean, what's time in this place anyway? But in the long run, we want to spend a lot of our eternity with each other."

"That sounds pretty cool," Kelsie agreed. "I think that may be a plan for Noah and I. We haven't really talked about the future since we got here. It's just too early to tell. I know he will want to do a lot of things, and so will I. But like you said, we've got nothing but time."

CHAPTER TWELVE

A s they neared the center of the city, the group of friends noted several large campuses, alive with activity, with expansive buildings and impressive facilities. Spires and towers extended far into the sky, many with windows made of cut rubies, emeralds and other precious stones. Some of these compounds appeared to cover many square miles. As they walked by the perimeter of one, they came upon the main gateway leading into the grounds. There, they saw two large signs on each massive gate post that read *THE GUILD OF SCRIBES.*

As they were standing there pondering the sign, a tall young man in knickers, a white ruffled linen shirt and a long coat walking into the campus stopped and asked, "Is there something I can help you with?"

"Yes, actually there is," Tilly replied. "We are newcomers on our way to The Thrones, but we've noticed several places like this and wondered what they were."

The young man nodded and smiled. "You mean the Guilds," he replied.

"The Guilds?" repeated Kelsie quizzically. "What are The Guilds?"

"The Guilds are places where individuals can pursue their interests," answered the young man. "There are Guilds for Art, Music, Sports, Culinary interests, Building, Engineering . . . you name it. You can work alongside some of the greatest names in your desired field. Experts both well known and unknown. It is an excellent opportunity. This is, as you can see, The Guild of Scribes."

"And may I ask what The Guild of Scribes is?" Christine countered.

The young man gave her a slight bow. "Certainly, my lady. The Guild of Scribes is a place where men and women meet to learn, discuss and record History, Literature and Scripture, with an emphasis on God's role in our lives, past and present."

"It kind of seems academic at this point," Edgar said. "I mean, no offense, but what difference does that sort of thing make at this stage in the game?"

"It is purely academic, in the best use of the word," agreed the man. "In fact, it is learning and sharing for learning and sharing's sake. That, and to glorify God, of course. Many who love knowledge come here to share and expound that knowledge. It is highly philosophical and educational, somewhat like the ancient Greeks; which is ironic, because some of the ancient Greeks spend a lot of time here. Others include teachers, preachers and lifelong students. For some, it may sound tedious, but others like me, it is actually a very enjoyable pastime."

"Well no offense, but does everybody here dress like that?" Noah asked, gesturing to the man's outfit.

He laughed. "Of course not, but I understand your confusion. I'm just a little more comfortable in these clothes. You have to understand, these were quite stylish in the Jamaican Colony, before I came to New Jerusalem."

Realization sunk into the group as Edgar asked the question they all wondered. "When did you, um, come over?"

"1762," was the man's response. "I was a clerk for a trading company. I would like to tell you that I succumbed to some exciting demise, such as a duel with a privateer or an attack by savages, but I'm afraid it was just a case of malaria. I always loved to read about adventures in the New World, until I finally got the chance to go there. I was in Kingston for only six weeks until sickness gave me the chance to see a new world that made the one I had always dreamt about pale in comparison. By the way, Elias Wheaton's the name," he added, extending a hand.

They all took his hand and introduced themselves in kind, giving Elias a thumbnail sketch of their former lives. He seemed genuinely pleased to meet 'such a fine group of Colonial Yankees', as he referred to them. As they were chatting with the former clerk, a boy about Jessica's size passed them with a purposeful stride, obviously focused on some important task. They had seen several of these children, all dressed in simple white robes with bare feet, all beautiful in appearance, and all seemingly absorbed with some sort of mission.

"Not meaning to change the subject," Jessica began, "but I've noticed several kids like him," she said, pointing at the boy that had passed them on his way. "There's something different about them. Are they angels?"

"Ah, the Emissaries," Elias replied. "No, my dear, they are not angels. They are something quite different. Those are the children who were never born. They are the ones whose lives were cut short by miscarriage or abortion. They are special because they are sons and daughters of man who have never and will never be touched by the sin and pain of the other side. They are uniquely virtuous, and so they serve God directly as messengers and representatives."

Kelsie was awed by the concept. "I noticed that he had a key on a gold chain around his neck; but they all don't wear one. What's the significance?"

Elias gave her a slightly sad little smile. "Very astute, Miss Kelsie," he said. "That means he is here because his life was aborted by someone. The children that are lost by their mothers due to miscarriage are here because God, in His infinite wisdom, chose for them to remain here. Each child that has a key however, was intended to do some work on the other side. They hold some answer to a prayer, perhaps more than one, inscribed on that key. Some were meant to cure a disease or become great leaders; others may have raised a beautiful family, still others may have led their own parents to the Lord. But their mission was cut short by a selfish, misguided, murderous act. So they wear the key to remind them that even though God always answers prayers, those on the other side sometimes reject God's gifts before they are opened."

"Does it hurt them to know that?" Tilly wondered aloud.

"God Himself is the only parent they have ever known," Elias answered. "They have more love and care than the best earthly mother or father could ever hope to provide. What do you think?"

"It almost sounds merciful that they didn't have to live on the other side. That's what I think," Edgar replied.

Elias gave him a quick glance. "Just because they are better off, never mistake the sinful butchering of innocents as a merciful act," he said quickly. "These children were created for a purpose, and that purpose was circumvented by the selfish sin of others. Certainly this was no surprise to God, for He knows all. But just because He knows of the sin that will be committed by all men doesn't mean He's not grieved by it. Not only was the opportunity to enter the other side taken from these young ones, every soul they may have touched was deprived of the gift of these little ones as well."

Edgar's eyes dropped as he studied Elias' words. "I understand, of course. It's just that I know many of these children would have probably faced difficult lives. Poor families, teen mothers; so many kids in our times are ignored, pulled from pillar to post and some are physically abused. They just endure a lot."

Tilly smiled as she put her hand on Edgar's shoulder. "We all endure a lot. Life's good, but it's tough. It's not fair, but we're the ones that made it that way. God has a plan for us, and we make a mess out it."

Jessica agreed. "Tilly's right. I was sick for a long time and I'm really glad it's over. But I'm still glad I got to be on the other side. I'm glad I had a mom and dad and sister. I'm glad I got to go to school and make friends. It gave me somebody to look forward to seeing again and it makes me appreciate the cool things about Heaven."

Edgar stroked Jessica's cheek. "You win, sweetie," he said with a smile. "Besides, we of all people know it's all just temporary. It doesn't make any difference if you're eight or eighty. It all passes away. I'm just glad I'm here."

"Me too," Christine said, wrapping her arms around his waist. "I would have been really mad at you if you hadn't made it."

They all shared a little chuckle. "Well, it's been good to meet you all, and I'm sure I'll see you again, but I see a friend coming up the way that I want to catch," Elias said. "Farewell and Godspeed. May your meeting at The Thrones be everything you have ever dreamed and more," he said, as he gave them a wave and turned up the road into the guild and called to his friend.

"Check it out," Noah said, gesturing to the pair.

Elias' friend was a man with skin that was nearly jet black and dreadlocks that hung halfway down his back. The travelers watched as the pair met, shook hands, and walked away having an animated discussion. "Now there goes an interesting pair of ex-Jamaicans. Talk about bringing people together . . . this place does it like no other," Noah grinned. "Come-on, *Mon*, let's get going," he winked to the group, in his best Jamaican accent.

CHAPTER THIRTEEN

They had noticed for some time that as they drew nearer the center of the city, the light grew steadily brighter. For the last few miles, it had seemed so bright, that if the group had not been bestowed with new eyes, it would have seemed almost unbearable. Fortunately, they all knew at this point, that they could have looked directly into the noonday sun without suffering any damage, and could have no doubt picked out the sunspots and flares occurring on its surface.

As they walked, they talked about how they should not be alarmed at being separated. They had all become friends during the journey together, but they also knew that they were approaching their destination, and that whatever came after this would probably mean that they would go their own way, at least for a season. They would no doubt see each other again, since they had eternity to spend together in this place, but there would be people to see and things to do that would take each of them down different paths.

Kelsie and Noah talked about this at some length. They had decided that they wanted to spend time together, much as Edgar and Christine had. But they both knew that their lives would probably take separate paths for a while. They decided that when they were ready to meet, that they would go to the gate at Reuben Way and wait for each other. If they couldn't wait, they would leave word with the Serbian street vendor. It wasn't the best plan, but Noah and Kelsie decided that if God had brought them together to make it here, it would work out the way He wanted.

That was another thing that was on Noah's mind. What did God want? Since he had been here, Noah had seen many people fulfilling their personal desires and ambitions, but there was a nagging thought in the back of his mind. What does God want us to do? Jesus gave His life for us; now do we just come here and do what we want, or is there a higher calling? Noah didn't know. But one thing he was sure of, although he didn't speak of it with anyone, not even Kelsie. If God has something He wants me to do for Him, I intend to do it.

As the group came within the last few miles of The Thrones, the bright light that they had been following took on a greenish glow. People began to slow down and bask in the warmth of its light. The luminance was almost tangible, as if they had stepped into a rainbow and were being showered by its light. As they drew closer, the reason for this sensation was apparent.

To their left, the buildings fell away, leaving a marvelous expansive green space that led down to a river bank. The river they were walking along came from a predictable source. It flowed from The Thrones.

The Thrones sat elevated above a huge fountain of crystal clear water. They appeared to be resting on a platform of solid crystal that was suspended above and by the flow of water from the fountain head. As the water splashed out, the resulting mists combined with the brightness coming from The Thrones, creating a multi-hued emerald rainbow that bathed the huge surrounding square in its light.

The waters flowed outward into a narrow deep lake that in turn became the broad, beautiful river that traveled between Rueben Way and Judah Road. On each side of the river grew large spreading trees, laden with gorgeous translucent fruit. The roots of each tree reached down the banks into the depths of the clear cold water, where they all joined as one living organism. Thus, even though they had the appearance of many, these were in fact the shoots of one great tree. The group drew near the river.

"The River of Life," Tilly breathed, with reverence and awe in her voice.

"The Tree of Life," Christine said, as her eyes sparkled with the joy of the moment.

"Can we touch the trees?" Kelsie asked. "Can we eat the fruit?" she inquired, looking around at her friends.

"To the one who is victorious, I will give the right to eat from the tree of life, which is in the paradise of God," Edgar said, quoting Revelation 2:7 (NIV).

That was all Kelsie need to hear. She ran through the thick grass of the river bank until she came to the nearest tree. She reached out and tugged at a softball sized fruit, with a thin skin like a plum, and a hue that was blushed with pink and yellow. It yielded easily to her, and after feeling the warm heft of it in her hand for a moment, she took a bite. Warm sweet nectar dribbled down her chin as she tasted something that had been unavailable to man since shortly after the beginning of time. It was more than just the taste; it was the experience, the almost audible thrumming of life essence as it coursed from the fruit into every cell of her being. Only then, only when Kelsie swallowed her first morsel of that fruit did she realize how very much mankind had missed out on.

She realized that Adam and Eve had stood in the first garden, like innocent children and listened to one that was in a sense, the original child molester. One who lured them away from the safe haven of their home, their life and their Father. Lucifer had stolen this from them and caused them to be wounded and abused, physically, emotionally and spiritually. He had stolen their birthright, their security, their life. Like many who have been abducted, mankind had come to accept this, and developed a warped kind of Stockholm syndrome in relationship to

Satan. They had come to accept him and the scraps he had thrown them as love and provision. In doing so, they missed out on this place, this ambrosial living fruit, this sense of life . . . and the presence of their Father. She looked up from fruit in her hand at The Thrones.

As she looked toward The Thrones, she could see there were three. Upon the center seat sat a figure that was the source of light within this land. He was exceptionally bright, exceptionally beautiful, and unlike any preconceptions she ever had of what God looked like. There were no wizened wrinkles, no long white beard or thick bushy brows. The amazing thing was that although she could see Him plainly, she couldn't even begin to describe Him. In fact, when talking much later with others, they all agreed that each one of them knew exactly what God looked like. They just couldn't begin to put it into words.

Seated at God's right, there was another figure. This individual looked very familiar to Kelsie. This was the One she and Noah had followed through the doorway. This was the Son of David, the Lamb of God, the Bright and Morning Star. He also shined with great brilliance. His hair was thick and white, like wool. His eyes appeared to be like fire and His robe was so white, it had a glow of its own. His smile was dazzling and He was looking at the thousands that surrounded Him with love and compassion that was deeper and more profound than anyone of them had ever seen.

The third seat was empty. At first Kelsie didn't know what this meant, and then it occurred to her. *This is the place for the Holy Spirit. He dwells among and within men now.* It also occurred to her that there would be a day when He would take His place with the Trinity. On that day, there would be no more conviction, no more need to walk with man, no more need to lead people and reveal Christ to the masses. On that day, the work would be finished.

As Kelsie soaked the scene in, she realized that something was different. She looked around for Noah, but he wasn't there. She looked to her traveling companions, but they were focused on the crowd and something that was up ahead. It was then that she saw what they were looking at. Noah had broken into a sprint and was running as fast as he could toward The Thrones.

CHAPTER FOURTEEN

Noah ran as fast as his new legs would take him toward The Thrones of God. He was overwhelmed by God's presence. Nothing, absolutely nothing mattered to him as much as being here, he realized. He had been created for this moment, drawn to this place from conception until now. Every step, every misstep, every breath and every heartbeat had taken him down this road to this spot. This was his destiny; to stand before the King. He felt totally and completely fulfilled. *If this is all there is, it is abundantly more than enough,* he thought.

He waded as deep into the crowd as he could, stepping around those who were kneeling and lying on their face in worship. By the appearance of some of the styles of garments represented, it was apparent that some of the people may have been there for centuries. They worshipped in a massive wave of prayer, praise and honor. As the masses spoke words of honor and glory that sounded like the waters of the ocean, branches of lightning and thunder crashed around The Thrones in a spectacular display of supernatural fireworks.

Above all of this, two angelic beings that Noah recognized as seraphim hovered over The Thrones, soaring upon one pair of their broad majestic wings, while they covered their faces with a smaller pair of wings. Still another set of wings covered their feet as a sign of humility. They spoke with voices that would have registered on the Richter scale, as a deep rumble proclaimed, "HOLY, HOLY, HOLY! LORD GOD ALMIGHTY! WHO WAS AND IS AND IS TO COME! THE HEAVENS AND THE EARTH ARE FILLED WITH HIS MAGNIFICENT GLORY!"

Shouts of "AMEN!" rose from the crowd as a mighty responsive chorus, while others sang songs both new and very ancient in a hundred languages. Noah could understand every word. As he drew near to the crystal dais upon which The Thrones were placed, he felt the weighty presence of God's glory and the magnetic gravity of His proximity. He had to get closer.

In front of the platform, was placed the Altar of solid gold, with a brilliant eternal flame burning upon it. On either side of the Altar were censors filled with incense that gave off a cloud of multicolored vapors. The vapors whispered, wept and shouted with many voices, as they vocalized the prayers of millions of those still on the other side. As the voices spoke, the Father would frequently raise a hand, and at His gesture, an Emissary would appear at His side to receive a quick message, just as quickly, be on their way, fulfilling a mission from God.

Before the Altar, sat the actual Ark of the Covenant. The ark made by Moses and Aaron on the other side was a faithful replica, made according to specifications given my God Himself. There were two glaring differences that Noah noticed however. First, this one was actually much larger. It was in fact, almost big enough to house a bus. Second, where the ark that was made by human hands was covered in gold and protected by the images of two cherubim on the cover of the box, the actual Ark was protected with two actual cherubim sitting on each end of the lid, with wings outstretched over its length. Their four faces peered about fiercely, as they repeated the worship call of the seraphim in unison.

Noah made it to the corner of the Ark nearest to the Throne of Christ, before falling to his knees. He raised his hands to Jesus and looked into that amazing, compassionate face, as something between a shout and a whoop of sheer wonder filled his lungs. His heart felt so full that it might explode, yet it seemed to grow within his chest, filling with the love of Christ. If he could have cried, his face would have been covered with tears. But the time for tears was over . . . forever. His cup was running over, not in a trickle, but in a torrent.

As he looked upon Jesus, he realized that Christ looked so unique, so new, and yet so familiar. His features seemed to combine every race and every culture known to man. Where Noah had seen pictures that depicted Jesus as Caucasian, African, Palestinian, and even Asian, he found the Lord to look like all of them; and yet He looked like none of them. He both met and exceeded the expectations of all, in appearance, presence, and depth of love. His interaction with The Father was so fluid and so connected, he finally understood how God could be both singular and triune in nature. As a man's body, mind, and spirit are completely connected, so was the Father, Son and Holy Ghost God in whose image man was made.

Noah was close enough to see that the scars upon the feet of Jesus were still there. Fresh and deep, they were clearly visible. Likewise, as Christ reached to take His Father's hand, Noah could see the scar that marked the Savior's wrist, deep between the two bones of His forearm. While they no longer hurt, no longer revealed any damage to the glorified body, the scars stood out as an eternal reminder to the price paid for the lives of God's adopted children. *I have graven you on the palms of my hands,* Noah mouthed the words to himself.

As his eyes fell to the hem of Jesus' robe, he saw that a swath of the brilliant white linen was stained dark with a deep red liquid. It was still wet, still shining, still . . . alive. *The life is in the blood*, Noah heard himself thinking. This was the Blood of Christ. The most precious substance known to man; it was the sacrificial price that brought us here, that brought us to Him. "OH, MY LORD AND MY GOD!" Noah cried in a loud voice as he fell on his face before Jesus.

As he lay there, Noah felt a warm hand on the back of his head, softly stroking through the thick brown curls of his hair. "Well done," he heard, as Jesus whispered softly into his ear. "Well done, Noah. You have made it home. You have fought the fight and you have been faithful over the few precious things I have blessed you with; your friends, your family, your talent, your ability. You have made the most out of it, putting loved ones before the material things of the other side and Me above all. You have done your best within the limitations of the dust from which you came. You have served me well as a child, as a brother and as a friend. Your sins have been washed away and you have been perfected in the sight of your Father. Enter into the rest of your Lord."

Noah felt the ultimate paradox in that singular moment. The immense gravity of the love of God was met by the incredible lightness of knowing that every burden, every sin, every worry was gone forever. *If I lay here forever, feeling like this, that's enough of Heaven for me,* he thought. His soul was overwhelmed by every praise and worship song and hymn he had ever heard. Every scripture verse he had ever read or listened to came through his mind in clear perfect recall. It was as if his complete service to Christ, every word, every thought, every moment, was downloaded and simultaneously laid at the feet of Jesus.

Noah laid there for a long time; how long, he had no idea. He just let the love, the praise, the presence and the experience flood over him in waves. He would speak and shout and sing. Sometimes he would get to his hands and knees and just respond with 'AMEN!' in unison with thousands of others as the seraphim and cherubim spoke their pronouncements of worship. Then, he would just lie back down and bask in the warmth of God's love. He didn't know what had happened to his friends, but he knew if they were here, they were fine. As for him, Noah never wanted to leave.

CHAPTER FIFTEEN

After Noah had laid there for what seemed like forever, he felt a hand on his shoulder, as a child spoke to him, obviously trying to get his attention. "Noah," the child said, "You need to come with me." Noah looked up at the child and saw that he was an Emissary. He was a boy with dark brown curls that looked much like his own and large brown eyes, with a slightly broad nose, peppered with freckles. His expression was serious, but not anxious or irritated. Since he wore no key around his neck, Noah knew that he was a child that had naturally been taken by God, not cut down by human intervention.

"What do you want?" Noah asked. "Does God have something He wants me to do? Whatever it is, I'm ready and available," he said, bowing on his knees, his curly hair touching the golden paving bricks.

"Please, don't do that," the Emissary said. "Don't bow to me. I'm just a person, like you," he said, shifting uncomfortably, "and yes, God has something for you to do."

Noah rose to his feet, looking at the boy with excitement. "What is it?" he asked. "I'm ready to go."

The boy smiled. There was something oddly familiar in that smile. Noah almost felt like he should know this little boy. "Actually, God wants you to take some time and experience this world. Get to know it, fulfill your dreams and ideas. These things glorify God, because they reveal His creative power, mercy and abundant provision. He takes great pleasure in watching His children enjoy this place."

Noah nodded slowly, not fully grasping. "Is that all?" he asked. "I mean, I know everyone seems to get to do what they want, but I thought God might have something special in mind. That's kind of what I had hoped, anyway." He seemed almost a bit disappointed.

"Your hopes will be realized, Noah. There will be specific things that God will ask of you at some point. When He is ready, He will send me to give you instructions. In the meantime, doing what you want to do is actually doing what God wants you to do. Does that make sense to you?" he inquired.

Noah agreed. "Sure. It just sounds so simple."

"It is simple," the Emissary replied. "But the things you will accomplish . . . well, those things are pretty incredible."

"Where do I start?" Noah asked the boy, while at the same time asking himself the same question.

"You will have a guide that will show you around. Someone you knew on the other side that gets to give you a tour of the city and counsel you about your plans," said the boy, as he took Noah's hand and began to lead him from the square. "I will take you to him now."

"I kind of got the idea you might show me around," Noah said. He had been trying to put his finger on the impression that he knew this child. Impossible, he thought. This boy was never born.

"No, I'm afraid not. But I am the Emissary assigned to you and when God sends for you, I'll always bring the message to you. My name is Benjamin," he said, with a slight bow.

Noah was thunderstruck by the realization that hit him. "Benjamin," he repeated the boy's name. Now he examined him in a different light. The boy had hair like Noah, big brown eyes and a nose similar to Lindsey Jo's. A dimple in his left cheek; a thin top lip and a full bottom lip. Because he appeared nine or ten years old at the most, Noah had gotten the context wrong. This boy wasn't younger than Noah; he was older. And the reason he looked familiar was because he and Noah were related. "Benjamin," he said again, "You're my brother, aren't you?

Benjamin grinned with the same open, toothy smile that characterized every picture Noah had ever seen of his sister. "This is Heaven. We are all brothers, Noah," he said, in a slightly mischievous tone, "But if you're asking if I am the son of Phillip and Sheri as well, then the answer is yes."

"Wow," Noah said, soaking in the reality of that statement. He was stunned. "I knew that Mom had a miscarriage before I was born, but I didn't think about seeing you here. I mean, I hate to say it, but I just hadn't considered it."

"It's okay," Benjamin said as they walked along. "I don't think a lot of families do. Some parents think about it, I imagine, but its hard to form an emotional attachment to a sibling you've never seen. But if you want, we can get to know each other."

"Well, yeah, "Noah replied, "Of course I do. I always thought it would be cool to have a brother." He looked at Benjamin again. "We really do look like brothers, you know? I mean, Lindsey Jo and I look like brothers and sisters, but you're kind of like a combination."

Benjamin got quiet for a moment. "What are they like? The rest of the family, I mean. What was it like growing up with them? I know I have a mother named Sheri and a father named Phillip and a sister named Lindsey on the other side. And I have you here . . . but I really don't know any details." He gave Noah a wistful, curious look.

Noah smiled at the memories that flooded his mind. "Well first of all, it's not just 'Lindsey' . . . it's 'Lindsey Jo'. You never leave the 'Jo' off.

She's fantastic. She's two years older than me, pretty, funny and very outgoing. She went to college, and by now, I guess she has graduated. She's married to a really smart guy named Bryant. You'd like him. He's got a razor sharp wit and loves her very much. Lindsey Jo and I were so close we were almost like twins. She always knew what I was thinking even before I said it. I can't wait to see her again . . . and I can't wait for her to meet you," Noah said, giving Benjamin an appreciative glance.

Noah continued. "Sheri is very strong, very determined," he said, faintly aware that he had referred to his mother as 'Sheri', instead of 'Mom'. "She's actually much stronger than she thinks she is. She was a great mom to me and took good care of us all. Personality wise, we are a lot alike. She always thought she never measured up, and I guess I've felt that way, even though I can see know that it wasn't true. Not for her; not for me."

Benjamin was fascinated. "What about Phillip? What is our dad like?" he asked.

"Phil is a big old teddy bear," Noah said with a smile. "Sometimes he's a little gruff, but he's really a very gentle, loving guy. He taught me a lot about a lot. Car stuff, music, you name it, we did it together. I guess he was one of the best friends I ever had. We sat up and talked for hours a lot of nights. I'll be glad when I get to see him again. I'll be glad to see them all again. I know they have a life on the other side, but I can't wait for them to get here."

Noah told Benjamin several stories about the family and about the place where he grew up. Since Benjamin had never been to the other side, he had no concept of the challenges and difficulties of a mortal life, but he enjoyed hearing about how his own family had overcome many struggles. As they walked together, he felt elated to meet his earthly brother and learn of the others that he hoped to see someday soon.

Finally, as Noah looked around, he realized that they had left the square and walked with several hundred others into one of several large reception pavilions on the outskirts surrounding The Thrones. He saw Emissaries walking with newcomers to meet others and making introductions. "Ben, where are we going exactly? Whom are we meeting? And do you know what happened to Kelsie, the girl that was with me?" he asked, a bit embarrassed that he hadn't inquired earlier.

"To answer your last question first," Benjamin began, "Kelsie is fine. She's with an Emissary and they are meeting someone to show her around, just like you are. As far as where we're going and whom we're meeting, you'll see soon enough. Normally, when a man dies, his father gets the honor of showing him around, if they both get to New Jerusalem. Since you skipped ahead of Phillip however, different arrangements for a guide have been made. In fact, there he is now," he said pointing to a young man standing about thirty yards from them.

The man was shorter than Noah by about four inches, with fine, jet black hair, combed straight back, in gentle waves. He had a dark complexion and pale green eyes, with a prominent nose and heavy brows that hinted of a Native American ancestry, and a thin distinctive black mustache. He was dressed in jeans, gold tipped boots, and a western shirt, with real pearl buttons. As soon as Noah saw him, he recognized the young man at once.

The black haired man with the mustache stepped quickly toward the Noah, pulled him into an embrace and gave him a big wet kiss on the cheek. "Hey Chief," Bud Wilson said, in a big grinning baritone. "What are you doing here this quick?"

CHAPTER SIXTEEN

he young mustached man that had once been Noah's grandfather hugged him tightly. Bud Wilson was very happy to see his grandson and tremendously honored to be called upon to show him around New Jerusalem. The last time he had seen Noah, he had only been a boy. Bud had always called Noah 'Chief', a personal nickname of his own device. Bud had referred to himself as 'Old Chief', his son Phillip as 'Big Chief' and Noah as simply 'Chief'. Now here was Noah, grown into an exceptional young man. He didn't know whether his new body was drastically altered in appearance from what Noah had looked like on the other side, but Bud suspected that Noah had looked pretty similar in his former life to the way he looked now. While years tended to slip away quickly, Bud knew that he hadn't been in Heaven very long. Noah had obviously passed over while still a young man.

Noah was overjoyed and awestruck at the appearance of his former grandfather. Noah found himself thinking of his guide as 'former' in the grandfather role, because it was apparent that they were now on equal footing. They were no longer grandfather and grandson; they were brothers. It was exciting for him to consider this. He had loved his 'Pa' as a child, but the memories of that sweet, deep voiced old man had faded in Noah's mind over time. Now Bud was young again. Noah thought of the stories he had heard about him; how years ago, Bud could break and ride horses with the skill of a rodeo performer, how he could jump a fence four feet high without touching it. *I can only imagine what you're capable of now,* he thought to himself.

"Chief, it's so good to see you!" Bud exclaimed. "I knew some of the family would be along soon enough, but I didn't expect to see you so soon. To be honest, I've been expecting your grandmother, Betty, or even your dad before you got here."

"I understand," Noah replied. "Nobody was more surprised than me." He explained what happened to Bud, and as he did, Bud interrupted him a few times, asking Noah to fill in the details about Kelsie, the accident and how it occurred. As Noah told his tale, Benjamin remained by his side, attentive to the story. Suddenly, Noah realized he hadn't made proper introductions. "Oh, hey, I'm so sorry, I forgot. This is Benjamin. He's uh, well, I guess in another life, he would have been my brother and another one of your grandsons."

Bud winked at Benjamin. "Well, thanks for the intro, but we already know each other, don't we Hon?" Bud said. He had retained lifelong habit of calling everyone, even men, 'Hon', as a term of endearment.

Benjamin smiled. "Of course we do. I looked Bud up when he first got here. He's the one that told me about you and the rest of the family.

Bud, Henry, and Slim have given me an idea of what the family tree looked like, but they didn't know what you were like as a grown man. But I think they will all be pleased to see the end result."

Noah knew that Slim and Henry were Bud's brother and father. While he had heard stories about them all his life, they died years before Noah was born. "Slim and Henry . . . will I get to meet them?" he asked.

"Sure," Bud replied. "We'll take you around and show you off. Slim and his boy Joe are still catching up, and I think they may be out in the hill country together right now, but I'll take you by and introduce you to Henry and Rebecca soon enough." Henry Wilson had built a nice home for himself and one for Rebecca, the woman that had once been his wife and Bud's mother. The homes were situated just outside the gate that led into Judah Road. There, just inside the gate, Rebecca ran a wonderful little café, serving fried fruit pies, light airy teacakes, and other delicacies she had perfected over a lifetime, as well as several she had mastered after reaching New Jerusalem. Henry divided his time between helping her and tending crops of strawberries, sweet potatoes, tomatoes, peas, and lentils, a vegetable unfamiliar to Henry until he came from the other side. Bud promised to take Noah there so that he could meet Henry and Rebecca for himself.

"But right now, I need to show you around the city," Bud continued. "There are places you need to see and people you will want to meet. As I'm sure you've already figured out, this is an amazing place; but God made it amazing because He is amazing and He rules an amazing people."

Noah turned to Benjamin. "Are you coming with us?"

Benjamin shook his head. "Sorry Noah, I've got to get back to The Thrones. But I'll see you again, hopefully soon. We may see each other around the city, and as I said, when the time comes for you to do a specific task for Him, I'll be the one that brings the message."

Noah found himself suddenly overcome by emotion. He had just met his brother a short time earlier, but I felt a connection to him that was obvious and significant. Noah dropped to one knee and hugged the boy tightly kissing him on the cheek. "I'm glad I got to see you, Ben. Take care of yourself. I love you, Bro," he said, running his fingers through Benjamin's curls.

"Me too," Benjamin replied. "I'm proud of you, Noah. I'm proud that you are here, and I can't wait until we can spend some time together. But right now, I think that Bud is anxious to show you around. He looks as though he's . . . how do you say it? 'Chomping at the bit.' That's it," he said with a smile.

Bud gave Benjamin a hug and a kiss on the forehead, before the boy waved goodbye to his kin and turned toward The Thrones. Noah and Bud watched him go. "I know he didn't have a chance to see the other side," Bud said, "But I'm glad that he's got the job he does. How awesome it is to know that he's always that close to God." He trailed off, lost in thought for a moment, staring into nothingness, before regaining his composure. "Well, Chief, let's go check this town out. We've got to take you to The Armory and then we can do the grand tour."

"The Armory?" Noah asked. "New Jerusalem has an armory? Why would we need weapons?" Noah was obviously puzzled.

"It's not what you think," Bud replied. "It's more of a symbolic gesture than anything. The weapons are very powerful, but we are armed as a symbol of God's strength, no weakness. Nobody will ever invade Heaven." He patted a small, ornate scabbard hanging at his side. Noah could see the jewel encrusted hilt of a sword protruding from it.

Now that Noah thought about it, almost everyone he had seen in New Jerusalem wore a sword at their side. He hadn't given it any thought before, but certainly everyone except newcomers was armed. Still, he was unclear as to the purpose. But if he got a sword out of the deal, he was only too happy to wear it.

As Noah and Bud walked along, they talked about the family. Bud listened closely, as Noah recounted the past several years of his life, Lindsey Jo's marriage, changes in Phillip and Sheri's life, and Betty's marriage to Duncan Jones, after Bud passed over. Betty had been Bud's wife for over fifty three years. She and Bud had built a good life together and raised three strong sons. Duncan was Bud's first cousin, and they had grown up very close. Duncan was a sweet gentle man that was kind to a fault. As a result, he had often been taken advantage of by those who saw his kindness and generosity as a weakness. At the revelation of their wedding, Noah was somewhat surprised when Bud just smiled and said, "That sounds just like Betty. She's always had the need to help somebody. Duncan never had a woman treat him right in his life, except for his momma. I'm glad they're happy." His answer was genuinely sincere.

Bud was happy to hear the news that Phillip had returned to college and built a new career, although he acknowledged the struggles associated with it. He was proud of Lindsey Jo and her accomplishments. Bud was glad that Sheri was doing well, in spite of the troubles that she had faced, including the loss of her father, only months prior to Noah's passing. "That girl is one of the strongest people I have ever known," he said.

Through Noah's discussions with Benjamin and Bud, he had discovered that the notion of loved ones in Heaven 'watching over' family members and knowing what was transpiring on the other side was erroneous. It would have been far too stressful and sorrowful on the residents of Heaven to see the difficulties and grief that their friends and families faced. While citizens of New Jerusalem might get to send an occasional message through a dream or some other indirect way, the people of Heaven and the other side were completely unaware of the events of each other's lives. While this was no doubt difficult for those still living the mortal struggle of the first life, it was an infinite blessing for those in the second life.

As they walked down the broad thoroughfare of Levi's Highway, they came in sight of an immense building, guarded by at least a legion of angels, holding long spears and large shields. The structure was supported by tall fluted columns, cut from solid jade, ringed in gold at the top and bottom. A detailed relief was emblazoned across the black granite façade of the front gable, depicting thousands of angels driving Satan and his demonic minions out of Heaven. The texture and depth of the images made the characters almost seem to live and move. Noah was awestruck at its terrific and ferocious beauty. "That is amazing. I've never seen anything like it," he breathed.

"Not surprising. It was carved as a joint effort between Michelangelo and Leonardo Da Vinci," Bud replied. "Those guys are pretty talented, huh?"

Noah grinned. "I think they'll do in a pinch," he said with a small chuckle. "Is this building what I think it is?" he asked anxiously.

"Yes, it is," Bud answered, with a broad, sweeping gesture of his hand. "This," he said, with a dramatic pause, "Is *the* Armory of God."

CHAPTER SEVENTEEN

T he halls of The Armory were covered with murals that told the stories of battles throughout the history of Earth. The interesting thing that caught Noah's eye however, was the fact that these images focused on angelic and supernatural intervention in various combat situations. One picture depicted an exhausted Revolutionary War patriot fighting valiantly as two angels, unseen by fellow combatants, supported him and guarded his back.

Another portrayed a lone Israeli tank patrolling the valley beneath the Golan Heights, while a Syrian invasion force waited to attack. The antagonists were confounded and confused by hundreds of angels whispering into the Syrian soldiers' ears, inciting fear and doubt.

Still another panorama illustrated the Philistine and Hebrew armies, opposing each other, as they all anxiously watched a standoff between a young shepherd and a towering figure in full battle armor. A massive formation of angels, unseen by the armies below, stood by in the sky above, to intervene if necessary. Noah knew of course, that the angelic support was never implemented in the conflict. Every child that ever attended Sunday school with any regularity knew how that story ended. The shepherd won; while the big man lost the fight, the armor, and his head.

There was a mural showing Michael the Archangel's conflict with Satan over the body of Moses; another depicted Michael's battle with the demonic prince of Persia, from the book of Daniel. As Noah and Bud approached the rear of the armory though, one painting stood out among the others.

There was a mural that covered the entire rear wall, describing an event that had not yet happened, but was already destined to occur. A wide Middle Eastern valley was filled with an innumerable international army, equipped with modern artillery, weapons, and air support. This army to end all armies was pitted against a tough, but rag tag and helplessly outmatched Israeli fighting force. But the focus of the huge multinational army was not on the Israelis. Their eyes, weapons and attention were riveted on the sky above.

In the sky over the Israelis was a bank of thick black clouds that filled the horizon. The clouds were lit with multiple lightning flashes and they poured immense raindrops and hailstones on the valley below. Riding on the brow of that storm, was a multitude that dwarfed the worldwide army that opposing them.

Millions upon millions of soldiers were mounted on stout, fierce warhorses that flexed their muscles as their hooves struck sparks from the tops of storm clouds. The soldiers were uniformed in white robes and armed with New Jerusalem swords. The army was divided into twenty four columns, each led by an elder of Heaven. Leading these elders and riding far out front, was the King of all Kings.

He was mounted upon a big white stallion and the King's eyes were ablaze with the righteous wrath of God. He looked exactly like Noah remembered Him, as though Jesus had posed for the portrait Himself. There was one stark difference, however. Where Noah had seen and felt nothing but love in Christ's gaze at The Thrones, His expression in the picture was one full of vengeance, fury and power.

Jesus carried no weapons, but the painting portrayed a wave of force that was evidently coming from His voice. The first wave of international troops had already fallen under the power of His words, as a black river of birds swirled downward to feed upon their flesh.

Noah soaked in the vivid imagery, the prophetic destiny of a history yet to come. In the army of God riding that rode through the clouds, he thought he recognized a couple of faces. In fact, he almost thought for a moment that he had seen his own.

"Impressive, ain't it?" said Bud, as he slipped his arms around Noah's shoulder. "I knew you'd love the artwork. They say a picture's worth a thousand words, but when I look at this, words just fail me." Noah simply nodded, as he continued to examine the detail of the painting, until Bud finally urged him to approach the long tables situated beneath the mural.

Each table was constructed of thick planks of rosewood, polished to a mirror like finish. The tables were approximately ten yards long and four yards wide. Noah guessed that there were hundred or more placed end to end.

Behind each table was a row of angels, providing armaments to the steady stream of newcomers forming five lines at each table. Behind the angels were racks containing thousands of swords and small hand carved boxes, no bigger than a man's palm.

As Noah and Bud approached the table, a broad shouldered angel with skin the color of caramel and luminous, light brown eyes addressed Noah, recognizing him as a newcomer. "Son of man," the angel said in a deep friendly rumble, "May I have your right hand please?"

Noah offered his hand, and the angel took it, closing his eyes and making a long, low, guttural sound that was like a cross between a purring cat and a low level earthquake. The angel's hand was very warm, almost hot to the touch. After a puzzling moment, Noah realized what the angel was doing. He was retrieving information.

Suddenly, the angel opened his eyes and looked at Noah. "Noah Issac Wilson, son of Phillip and Sheri, born the third of April, in the year of our Lord, nineteen hundred and ninety one."

"Uh, yeah . . . that would be me," Noah replied, blinking.

"Very good," the angel said, releasing Noah's hand. He turned and searched briefly among the small boxes on the racks behind him; until he found the one he was looking for and placed it on the table. The box was made of wood, covered with intricate carvings of vines, covered with plump bunches of grapes. In the center of the lid was a gold script that read *Noah Isaac Wilson, CHILD OF THE KING.* When Noah read the words, his heart nearly jumped out of his chest with excitement.

More than a year prior to the accident, Noah had entertained the thought of getting a tattoo. Inspired by the Christian themed ink worn by his close friend and co-worker, Bo, Noah had played with several ideas, but kept returning to one image in particular. The vision he kept seeing, drawing and thinking about was a stylized script bearing four words: *CHILD OF THE KING.* While he never got the tattoo, the image never left him. Now that exact image that he had drawn and dreamt about was inlaid upon the surface of the box before him.

The angel placed a hand on the side of the box and explained its contents. "Noah, this serves as your identification, as well as a symbol of God's grace and your position within the Kingdom of Heaven. In the vernacular of your time, you might think of this as your 'dog tags'. Millennia ago, when an accused person was brought up for judgment, the judge would hand down the verdict in the form of a small stone. A black stone signified guilt and condemnation, while a white stone represented innocence and liberty. Because of Christ's sacrifice and your dependence on Him, Jesus has promised to give you a white stone, with His own personal name for you written upon it. This is that personalized stone." He slid the box across the table, into Noah's hands.

Noah opened the box and found a brilliant white stone about an inch in diameter. A fine gold chain was threaded through a hole drilled in the center. The stone itself was opaque, with small gold letters circling its circumference just beneath the surface. Noah read the letters to himself . . . *Rea' Adam-El Yada' Mela'kah.* As he read the name, he knew the meaning instantly . . . *Friend of Man and God, Skilled in All.* He was overwhelmed by both the interpretation and the gravity of the words. This was what God thought of him. God considered Noah a friend, as well as a master of any work he chose to put his hand to. *Oh, that God would know me and think so much of me.* It was the most humbling thing he had ever experienced.

Noah looked at Bud. "Do you have one of these?" he asked, holding the stone in the palm of his open hand.

Bud smiled and tugged a chain at the edge of his collar. His stone popped free from beneath his shirt. "Sure. I keep it close to my heart," he replied in an uncharacteristically quiet tone, before slipping the stone back into its place.

Bud didn't ask Noah what his special name was. Likewise, Noah didn't ask Bud about the writing on his stone. They both understood that the stone and the special name was a personal, intimate token of love between each person and God.

As Noah slipped the chain containing the stone around his neck, the angel leaned on the table, palms down. "Now," he said, "We need to talk about armor. On the other side, the armor of God is composed of the principles of faith, truth, righteousness, salvation, and the gospel of peace. Since these elements have been fulfilled upon your arrival in Heaven, only one article is left; that article is your weapon. It is the ultimate weapon, more powerful than all the nuclear and conventional arsenals of history combined. What you are about to receive seems simple, but make no mistake; it is far more than a mere ornament worn at your side. It is the most devastating, deepest penetrating weapon known to men or angels." The angel turned and took a sword from the rack behind him. "This," the angel said, "Is your sword." He held the sword resting upon both open palms and offered it to Noah.

Noah looked at the sword, sheathed in a hand tooled, brown leather sheath. A few tasteful precious stones and spare gold trim inlaid in the scabbard and the hilt of the sword had a rich but subdued effect. The real treasure lay within the sheath.

He took the sword from the angel and was shocked at its lightness. The sword almost seemed to float; which explained, at least in part, how easily everyone carried these exquisite swords. He gripped the sheath with his left hand, and drew the blade out with his right.

The light caught the blade, as Noah examined it closely. It was a broad, double edged blade, made of metal that was as transparent as glass, and constructed in a manner similar to Damascus steel. Damascus steel was forged by hammering the metal into a wide thin sheet, folding it in half, and hammering it out again. This process was repeated multiple times, until the blade was forged as a laminate of many layers. Because of the tempering created by the heat and stress of the process, the outer layers of the blade would remain softer and pliable, while the center could be honed to a fine, tough, razor sharp edge. The surface of this sword revealed the fine lines of a similar design, but the depths of its finish revealed much more.

As Noah looked into the transparent blade, he could see tiny lines of text running the length of the sword, layer after layer, all the way to the center of the crystal clear metal. As he squinted a bit, the lines came into sharp focus. "For God so loved the world, that he gave his only begotten Son, that whosoever believeth in him should not perish, but have everlasting life (John 3:16, KJV)," read one line. 'Surely goodness and mercy shall follow me all the days of my life: and I will dwell in the house of the LORD forever (Psalm 23:6, KJV),' read another. Line after line, one after another; Noah read scripture after scripture.

"That's where the power comes from," Noah said aloud in wonder, as he held the sword upward and watched the light shine through it, projecting the lines of truth across the floor. "This is literally the sword of the Word of God."

CHAPTER EIGHTEEN

If Noah and Bud had been a few moments earlier, they would have seen two young ladies leaving the Armory. Following a substantial time spent at the feet of Jesus, in worship and fellowship with God, an Emissary had taken her to meet her guide. Kelsie had met up with a young lady named Betty that had once been the mother of Kelsie's mother. After a joyful, loving reunion, Betty led Kelsie to the Armory, where the tall, red haired newcomer had received her white stone and sword, before they headed out to see the city.

"Baby, you wear that blade almost too well," said Betty, eyeing the scabbard swinging from Kelsie's hip. "It kind of gives you a 'Jane of the Jungle' look," she added with a laugh.

Kelsie flashed her a brilliant grin. "Hey now, you're talking to a camo wearing, skeet shooting, four wheeling, genuine tomboy. I rock this sword," she said, as her long legs strutted out ahead a few steps, before putting her hand on her hip, looking back over her shoulder and tossing her long red mane. "And it's more of a 'Red Sonya" thing, don't you think?"

They both broke into giggles that proved difficult to tame. They were like two long lost friends, suddenly finding each other and catching up without missing a beat. With the time that Betty had already spent in Heaven, she had grown accustomed to being young again, which made it easier for the two of them to reconnect.

Like Noah's grandfather, Kelsie's grandmother had missed several years of her granddaughter's life, and seeing her as a grown woman was wonderful and thrilling. Kelsie was even more amazing than she could have imagined, with a glowing smile and personality that was accentuated by the build and height of a model. She could have been anything. Now, she could do anything.

Kelsie had told Betty about Noah, about the accident, and about the transition to this place. Betty nodded thoughtfully. "It was obviously meant to be. The way you both were drawn to each other, and especially with him waiting around for you," Betty said. "That doesn't happen very often. God let him do that because you two were intended to be together. What do you think he will do? From the sound of your voice, you two still have a future together."

"Oh yeah, there's more to come," Kelsie replied. "But we talked about this before we got to The Thrones. We knew there would be things to do and people to see. We've agreed to meet up again later. If we have things we want to accomplish, that's okay. We've got the time to do what we want, when we want, with whom we want. I'll see him again . . . and I think our eternities are linked. It just may be a little while. But I can't wait for you to meet him," she said, with a gleam in her eye.

As the duo, strolled out Asher's Avenue, Kelsie filled Betty in about the family, while Betty pointed out the parks, architecture, and fellow brothers and sisters enjoying their lives in New Jerusalem. They stopped across from an exquisite tower built of a dozen shades of diamonds. The light shimmered through the complex cut facets. Many of the stones were the size of a car. "It's spectacular," breathed Kelsie.

"It's coal," remarked Betty. "All it needed was time and pressure. Which is ironic, considering that we are originally made from dust. I guess time and pressure turns us into something better as well. That, and the breath of God," she added.

They studied the tower as they enjoyed a snow cone from a street side café. It was made from real snow, brought in from the mountains, and flavored with fruit juice. Betty ordered a cherry flavored one; Kelsie had one made with cobbler berries. She had gotten hooked on them during the journey to the city. The snow cones were cold, sweet and wonderful.

"Where are we going?" Kelsie asked the woman that had been her grandmother on the other side. She had been curious about the leisurely, yet purposeful path they had taken. "You seem to be taking me somewhere in particular."

Betty gave her a mysterious little smile. "Well, what would you like to do?" she asked. "Where would you like to go?"

"Well, you're going to think it's kind of strange," Kelsie began. "But a big part of my life on the other side was sports. I really enjoyed basketball, soccer, you name it. I was wondering . . . do we have anything like that on this side?"

Betty's expression tried to keep an inscrutable expression, but it was hard to keep the corners of her mouth from turning upward. "That's sort of what I thought. But don't ask any more questions. I want it to be a surprise. I think you will really like it though."

"Deal," replied Kelsie. She had to make a conscious effort to keep from guessing, because she knew that the enhanced mental capabilities of her new mind would reveal the answer, if she really felt she needed to know. *So, I'll just wait,* Kelsie thought. *I don't need to know . . . yet.*

As they continued on their journey, Kelsie struck up a conversation with a Celtic woman named Colleen that had passed over during the sixth century. She had been converted to Christianity from Druidism by monks that had braved the barbaric time and place where she lived to act as missionaries. Although she had understood very little about the Christ who had given His life for her, she had trusted in the truth of that act, and her simple faith had been enough. Since being here, she had learned much, and loved much. She commented on Kelsie's hair, and how it made her think of her best friend on the other side. "She was like a sister to me. So long ago," Colleen said. "And yet, it seems like yesterday."

Colleen explained that the friend had not shared in her faith, and thus, had not come to New Jerusalem. Kelsie asked how that made Colleen feel. "I know you would think that I would be a 'might sorrowful and think that God was being unfair," she said. "But strangely, I just understand. God is righteous and just, and she had the same chance I did. He did not send her away; she chose the other path herself. I wish she had not, but I cannot do a thing to make it different. Not even God could; He set the standard, and He cannot lie and does not change."

Kelsie thought it was interesting to hear Colleen speak of her thoughts about a loved one that did not make it to Heaven. She had thought about that sometimes on the other side, and she had heard different ideas on the subject. Some had said that people in Heaven would forget those that didn't make it; others claimed that individuals that made it might not even recognize each other. Now she knew that she would know those that made it and those that didn't, but God in His design had removed the sting of that pain and loss. You simply understood, without questioning. It was each person's choice.

While they were chatting, they lost track of time and distance. As a result, Kelsie was taken aback when the trio came to a cross street where the shops and homes stopped abruptly. Across the street was a vast campus that stretched from Asher's Avenue to Zebulon Road. It covered over a hundred square miles and was a mix of flat green fields laid out in a varying types of grids, buildings, multiple stadiums, and other venues. They stopped talking as Kelsie just looked wide eyed at the wide open area. She looked at Betty inquisitively. "Is this the surprise you had planned for me?" she asked.

"Yes, as a matter of fact, it is," Betty said, putting her hand on Kelsie's shoulder. "Track and field, swimming, volleyball, soccer, basketball, hockey, rugby, lacrosse, and probably a hundred sporting events you've never heard of. They even have automobile and motorcycle racing. There are champions here from ancient Olympians to Super Bowl, World Cup, Stanley Cup and World Series winners. Kelsie Bug, you are going to love it. This is the New Jerusalem Sports Complex."

Chapter Nineteen

uring the time that Kelsie was entering the New Jerusalem Sports Complex, Noah and Bud were standing on a huge transparent bridge shaped from a single block of flawless crystal that stretched a span of twenty four miles over the River of Life. The bridge was situated on Straight Street, a thoroughfare that crossed from Rueben Way to Judah Road, through rolling meadows, impressive mansions, shops and gardens. Noah and Bud had traveled down Judah Road, cutting across to back track Noah's original route into the city. Noah wasn't sure why Bud was going this way, but he certainly enjoyed the bridge and the view.

The river flowed broad and clear over a mile below their feet. The effect was as if Bud and Noah were standing in midair, looking down at the river. Although it was deep, the clarity of the water was such that Noah could see the river bottom of striated topaz, turquoise and amethyst. He could also see what appeared to be large shadows moving beneath the surface. Then suddenly, as the shadows changed direction, Noah would see a brilliant flash of metallic rainbows; they were huge schools of fish.

"This is beautiful," Noah said, putting his arm around Bud's shoulder. "I could have never imagined anything like this in a thousand years."

Bud smiled. "Eye hath not seen, nor ear heard, neither have entered into the heart of man, the things which God hath prepared for them that love Him," he replied. "But now you have; and you ain't seen nothing yet. This is a brave new world Noah, full of wonders, opportunities and dreams come true. Since I was a boy, I had heard the stories, sung the songs, even dreamed about it myself. But the human mind can't do it justice."

"No kidding," Noah said. "I cannot wait for Lindsey Jo to see this. Phil, Sheri, Bryant- this is going to blow their minds." He stopped, thoughtful for a moment. "It's going to be a long time before I see them again, isn't it?"

"Not as long as you think," Bud answered. "Jesus may go get them at any time. We've all been expecting it. They say when the city was young, folks figured it would be a long time, but look around you. It's nearly complete. But even so, if they live a long natural life on the other side, it won't seem that long to you. It almost seems like I just got here, but you've told me that eight years had passed before you showed up."

"But what about them?" Noah inquired. "It doesn't seem like a long time to us, but it's a lifetime for them. I know they hurt; I know they miss me. When I first got here, I was able to communicate with a friend of mine through a dream. Is there any way I can get a message to them to let them know I'm all right?"

Bud stepped back and looked at Noah. "As a matter of fact, there is. I'm proud of you, Chief. It's sweet of you to think of them in the middle of all this. You can't talk to them directly, of course. But you can send them a message. God gives us the ability to send things to them. It may be a breeze or a flower growing somewhere; little things to remind them of you and to let them know that you are okay. I've sent doves into your grandmother's backyard many times to let her know I was thinking about her."

Noah grinned. "That's pretty cool. How do you do it?"

"It's actually pretty easy," Bud replied. "Just think about whomever you want to send a message to, and really focus on them. Then, just think about whatever you want to send. Sometimes, it helps to reach out with your hands and pull things together with your will to control them. I can usually focus better that way. My suggestion is to stick to one or two things that you really like; something that says it's you. Then repeat it every so often. The repetition is what makes it seem like it's coming from you. A person may see a red bird for example and not think much of it; but if you see three in a day's time, it takes on a new meaning."

Noah considered this. *I need something that really personifies me*, he thought. *One of the most obvious things in nature that practically* spoke his name was a rainbow. "You think I can make a rainbow?" he asked Bud.

"You betcha," Bud said. "Just think about it and pull one together."

Noah turned and looked out at the river. He held out his right hand with eyes closed and began to focus on the colors. As he did so, he imagined the coolness and weight of different shades of violet, orange, blue, yellow and green gathering in his hand. As he heard a soft chuckle from Bud, he opened his eyes.

Colors were materializing from the light around them and falling into his palm, like the fibers of a rope. The strands of light draped from his hand and cascaded over the rail of the bridge down to the river below. He could actually feel the rainbow; light, but material, cool to the touch, thrumming in his hand, as if it were alive. His face broke into a huge involuntary grin. If I can do this, Noah thought, I might as well go two for two. He extended his left hand, palm up, and immediately, strands of multihued light began to gather there. The colors grew brighter and more substantial, until finally he closed his fingers and thumbs around them, gripping them like thick ropes of light.

Bud leaned in and spoke softly into his ear. "Now, throw them into the other side," he said.

Noah raised his hands over his head, hauling back on the twin rainbows quickly until they snapped thousands of feet into the air like giant whips. They were suspended there for only a moment, until Noah pulled them forward, like throwing a lasso. They coiled forward in a large double arc, as the ends pitched forward suddenly and pierced the sky above the horizon, disappearing from sight. As he felt their momentum tug on his hands, he let go and watched them pass through the sky of Heaven into the other side. "That is the coolest thing I've ever done," Noah said in slack jawed amazement.

The summer following Noah's passing, his friends and family mentioned seeing double rainbows multiple times. Double rainbows were reported on as news curiosities and even a major celebrity commented on Twitter about a double rainbow he had seen, wondering what it meant. For Noah's parents however, the message was clear. Noah and Kelsie had arrived at their destination and they were both doing well. Noah's message came through, loud and clear.

Bud and Noah continued on, talking about the many abilities that had been bestowed upon them by their new life in New Jerusalem. Bud told Noah how he had been able to summon doves and breezes to send to the other side. Noah said that he might add butterflies to his repertoire of messengers to the other side, since he had always found them ethereal and fascinating.

As they approached the intersection of Straight Street and Judah Road, Noah recognized where they were. The Guild of Scribes lay to his immediate right, with its impressive scholarly appearance and small groups of attendees strolling across its rolling lawns, deep in discussion. "I've been here before," Noah said. "We met a guy by the name of Elias. He has a cool story."

"Well I'm glad you've been here, because there's somebody here you'll want to see," Bud replied.

Noah looked at him quizzically. "Really? I mean, it's a fantastic place, but honestly, I can't imagine this being my sort of thing."

Bud grinned. "Don't be so sure," he said as they turned between the gate posts. "I wasn't much for this sort of thing when I was on the other side either. To be honest, Noah, I could barely read. But that's changed of course. I can read and speak any language that has ever existed, including angelic languages. I've spent quite a bit of time here. There's a lot of interesting people to talk to . . . and one in particular that will be glad to see you." He led Noah between two large structures into a beautiful commons area, supplied with benches and fountains beneath a canopy of spreading elms and oaks.

Situated at one of the benches were three young men, heavily engaged in conversation. One was seated, while the other two stood. The seated man was dressed in a long coat and a string tie, reminiscent of the late nineteenth century. He had a well groomed beard and dark, swept-back hair. The other two men were both fairly short in stature and clean shaven. Their clothing was a bit more contemporary. One of the shorter men was slightly stocky, dressed in a two piece suit and tie, with a shock of thick hair parted on the side and combed back. The other one was thinner, wearing light colored jeans, a knit sport shirt and a short cropped crew cut. Noah couldn't see the third man's face, because he was facing the other two. The bearing of all three men though had one thing in common; these men had the look of preachers.

"Grace, brothers, is the key," the bearded man was saying. "We sow what we reap, most assuredly, but only the grace of God gives us a crop such as this," he said, gesturing around him. "It took half my earthly ministry to understand that the Father hates sin, but loves in the sinner. Wouldn't you agree, Mose?"

The stocky one of the two shorter men responded with a slow, deep voice full of gentle thoughtfulness. "Dwight, I've said the same thing many times. In fact, I've quoted you a few times on the subject," he said with a short chuckle. "Denny and I spent a lot of time telling anybody that would listen and even some that wouldn't about the grace of God," he said, nodding at the thinner man with the crew cut.

With that remark, Noah suddenly felt a pang of recognition, staring at the back of the other man. "Denny?" he said aloud, suddenly aware of why Bud had brought him to this place.

The thin young man with the crew cut turned to face Noah, and even though he looked forty years younger and a hundred pounds lighter, his crooked little smile was familiar. Dennis Buttery, Noah's maternal grandfather that had passed only five months before Noah himself, looked at Noah, winked and said, "Hey Noah, long time no see."

CHAPTER TWENTY

Dennis Buttery grabbed his former grandson in a bear hug and buried his face in Noah's shoulder. It was a surreal experience for Noah, since Dennis had returned to the slight build and youthful appearance of his young adulthood. He looks more like a kid brother than a grandfather, Noah thought to himself. But he was very glad to see Dennis, or Denny, as his friends called him.

"Fellas, I've got a couple of guys I want to introduce you to," Dennis Buttery said with a grin. "This is Bud and Noah Wilson. Noah is my daughter's son."

The stocky young man in the two piece suit stuck out his hand. "I already know Bud," he said smiling and shaking Bud's hand. "I was his pastor for a few years. It's really a pleasure to meet you, Noah," he added, reaching out and putting his hand on Noah's shoulder. "Whose son are you? Bob's or John's?"

"He's Phil David's boy," Bud said. "He's the youngest of Phil's kids."

"Phillip's boy, huh? Well, I'm Mose Bryum. I knew your daddy when he was just a boy. It's hard to imagine him with grown children, but as they say, time flies."

Noah smiled at Mose and said, "I've got an older sister as well, that's married. She's still on the other side. I just got here."

Mose studied him for a moment. "You were still young when you got here, weren't you, son? I can see it in your demeanor."

"Not quite nineteen," Noah replied. "My girlfriend was seventeen. We got here together. It was a motorcycle accident."

Dennis shook his head. "Noah, you're going to meet a lot of folks that got here the same way. Those things are an accident waiting to happen. Unfortunately, not everybody's as prepared as you were when the time comes."

"But for those that are, it's a blessing," the bearded man said as he stood. "Nothing on the other side can compare with the wonders of Heaven. It's a pleasure to meet you, Noah. Moody's the name, Dwight Moody."

"I think I've heard my dad mention you," Noah replied. "Do they call you D.L. Moody, by any chance?"

Dwight smiled. "Mainly the book publishers on the other side. I think they were trying to save a few letters when they sent a book to the typesetters. It's just Dwight here."

While Noah hadn't read any of his books, he knew that Dwight had
been a famous preacher and author many years ago on the other side.
He had heard Phil mention Moody, even quote him during a sermon.
Likewise, he knew that Phil thought a lot of Mose Byrum, his
childhood pastor. This is so cool, he thought. To see Dennis, Mose and
Dwight, just sitting around, talking about the gospel. This must be an
awesome thing for those that have dedicated their lives to preaching.
But his mind switched gears suddenly when his maternal grandfather
spoke.

"Noah, have you and Bud eaten lately?" Dennis asked.

"No, but I'm always up for a bite," Noah replied.

"Then why don't we all go over to Haskell's?" Bud said. "I could
stand some country cooking."

"You all go on," Dwight said. "John is going to be down at
Redemption Hall, leading a forum on the contents of the Hidden
Revelation Scroll. If I get tied up with Haskell, I'll never get back. No
matter how many times I hear about the subject, I like to hear John talk
about it again. Good to meet you brothers," he said with a smile and a
wave, and headed across campus.

"When he says John, is he talking about the Apostle John?" Noah
asked Dennis.

"None other," Dennis said with a smile. "Several of the apostles come around here," he said. "Except for Peter, that is. I think he slips off and goes fishing every chance he gets," he chuckled.

Noah and the rest walked down to the gate and crossed the street to the other side of Judah Road. About a mile from the Guild was a side street that formed a kind of arcade of unusually humble looking shops and restaurants. While there were no 'hole in the wall' places in Heaven, these little places were as meager as Noah had seen. One of the eateries, with pristine white paint, rockers on the front porch and red gingham curtains, was identified by a stylized sign above the door that read simply, "*Haskell's*".

The tables were covered by red gingham tablecloths and the place was resplendent with cute little antique curios, a jukebox, and a red Coca Cola cooler along one wall. The smell of fried food lingered in the air, and for a moment, Noah almost felt like he was back on the other side. But this place is way better and cleaner than any little 'meat and three' diner I've ever seen, Noah thought.

The place was run by a tall, gangly young man with a prominent jaw named Haskell Akins. Haskell knew all the men that accompanied Noah, and had known Noah's parents on the other side. He had been a preacher and a farmer, but now that he was here in New Jerusalem, he had decided to try his hand at running a diner for a while. Haskell had always said with a smile, "I know there's got to be fried taters in Heaven." Now, he was doing his part to make sure.

The food was simple but amazing; smoked barbeque, white beans with a hot pickle relish known colloquially as 'chow chow', crispy cornbread and sizzling pan fried potatoes. As Noah listened to the group of friends berate each other with friendly banter and tell jokes that they had all heard a thousand times, he felt at home with these men. They were all the kind of men he had grown up with. A trio of others came in and dragged a table over to join them. Bobby, Harold and Donald sat down and began to chew the fat, laughing and talking over crystal mason jars brimming with sweet tea.

Noah recognized Donald as a much younger version of the old man that had lived down the road from his family when Noah was a boy. Even as an old man, Donald had been full of cheer, fun and jokes, but now he was in rare form indeed. Bobby and Harold, however, were unknown to him, although they apparently knew Bud quite well. One had black hair and a dark complexion, while the other was fairer skinned, with sandy blonde hair. Something about him seems familiar, Noah thought. Then, a thought occurred to him.

Harold Briley and Bobby Hodges had been best friends since they were children. Growing up in the same small community that Noah's family came from, they had worked together, played together, and went to church together, as children, teens and men. They had raised families and buildings together, working as carpenters and farmers. Then one sunny day, they had hooked up the boat and went fishing together.

When their bodies were found, it was believed that Bobby had suffered a heart attack, since no water was found in his lungs. Harold had drowned, and the boast was circling where they drew their last breath on the other side. While it was unclear which one tried to save the other, the end result was evident. They had died as they had lived; best friends until the end.

Bobby's youngest child, Angie, was only twelve when he passed away. He had no way of knowing that his daughter had two children, a girl and a boy. That girl, Bobby's granddaughter, was Kayla, Noah's former girlfriend.

"Say, is your last name Hodges?" Noah asked Bobby.

"Yup, sure is," The sandy haired man said. "Why do you ask?"

Noah grinned. "I've spent a lot of time in Hodges Hollow. I know your family; your wife, kids and grandkids. I dated your granddaughter, and worked with your son," he replied.

Bobby got a wistful look in his eyes, as he chewed a bite of cornbread. "How are they?" he asked. "What are they like? It's been a long time. I've never seen some of them."

"They are doing as well as anyone on the other side," Noah said plainly. "Life's hard there. You know that. But they are good people; the salt of the earth, as they say. I've spent a lot of time with them. I love them all; especially Kayla. That's your granddaughter; she is Angie's daughter."

"Angie's daughter," Bobby Hodges repeated. "It almost doesn't seem possible. She was pretty much still a kid the last time I saw her."

"Well, she's got two children now," Noah replied. "Blake is her son. He's the youngest. Kayla is nearly eighteen, and as cute as they come. She's short and petite, with blonde hair and green eyes. In fact, anybody got a pencil and paper?"

"Hang on a second," Haskell said. He scrambled around in the kitchen for a moment and came out with a sheaf of crisp, white paper and a thin, sharp pencil of solid graphite.

Noah took the pencil and paper, and as Bobby, Denny and Bud watched, he began to sketch the outline of Kayla's face. He penciled in the eyes, the lashes and the nose. He shaded in the curve of her lip, and put a light in her eyes that gave the drawing a lifelike appearance. As he completed each detail, the color of the pencil tip changed at will, allowing him to produce an image in full color, as he recalled her countenance. While Noah had been quite the artist on the other side, his talent had obviously been augmented by his transition into Heaven.

The portrait had a three dimensional quality, with an extremely high definition of detail. "There she is," Noah said, as he finished with a flourish and turned the picture so Bobby could view it.

Bobby studied both the drawing and Noah for a long moment. "You say you dated her?" he asked.

"For about three years," Noah said. "I loved her, Bobby. I still do. We were close; in fact, we talked about a future together. In the end, it just didn't work out. We still cared about each other, but it seemed like God had other plans for me. Now, I realize that it worked out for the best. I just pray she's okay and that she finds happiness. She deserves it. Kayla's a good girl and I want the best for her."

The group fell silent and listened as Noah continued talking about Kayla, Blake, Angie, and the rest of the family. Bobby, Donald and Harold listened with interest as he talked about working with Kayla's Uncle Randy, framing houses together. He talked about how he had met Kelsie and how he had tried to make the breakup with Kayla as easy as possible, but the complications of relationships had left wounded hearts and hard words. "It's so hard on the other side, you know? You love people and you don't want to hurt them, but you don't know how to figure all that junk out. I'm so glad that part of life is over for me," Noah said.

He told them how he had been drawn to Kelsie and how it was obviously God's plan for them to meet and become an integral part of each other's lives. Noah told the men about the day he died, about the accident and how he and Kelsie had stepped over into Heaven together. "We're going to meet up again, later. She and I have a lot to do together."

The men smiled and agreed. "There's plenty of time now to do what you want, with whomever you want," Dennis said. "All the troubles and all the heartaches are worth it, Noah. I can't tell you how many tears I've cried and how hard I worked to try to keep a little flock together for God on the other side. I've been so disgusted and so discouraged I wanted to give up. But this land is so sweet and so good; it's better than I ever imagined."

As Noah looked around the table at all these men that had once been old and tired, and now were young and vibrant, he only smiled and nodded. Taking a long sip of cold sweet tea from a mason jar and stuffing a bite of smoked barbeque into his mouth, Noah considered the jeweled walls, streets of gold, and realized that a simple meal with a bunch of good old country boys was just as precious. *Yeah, it's better than I ever imagined too,* he thought.

CHAPTER TWENTY ONE

"Ugh! GET OFF ME!" Kelsie shouted with a fierce grin, as she drove her shoulder into the chest of her opponent in a playful, but aggressive tone. While the competition was good spirited, when Kelsie was on the basketball court, she played to win. Her offensive move pitched the young man that was playing one on one with her off his feet, sliding across the boards nearly out of bounds. Using her momentum, she spun on her toe, and went for a lay-up, as the ball swooshed through the net. "And that's a game—100 to 87. I believe I win this one," she said with a smile.

"I'm pretty sure if we'd had a referee, that last move would be called a personal foul," the young man said, propping himself up on an elbow. He was tall and wiry, with a tangle of unruly dark hair and deep set eyes.

Kelsie offered him a hand. "Oh, quit whining Abe, and take it like a man," she said, pulling him to his feet. "Besides, I thought we didn't need referees in Heaven."

"With moves that like, maybe we should start," he said sheepishly. "Red, you've got to be one of the toughest girls I've ever run across."

He blushed, still a bit uncomfortable in the presence of strong women, even after all these years. He had always been somewhat shy around females, which was surprising, given his history.

Kelsie looked at the somewhat awkward young man, and thought about the surreal circumstance of their surroundings. Here she was, in Heaven, playing a friendly game of one on one, with possibly one of the most unlikely competitors she could have imagined. The young man, that honestly looked more like a gangly teen, was a good athlete. He wasn't conventionally handsome, but he had a distinctive and familiar look. He had a bit of a lantern jaw, prominent, busy brows, sallow skin and hair that looked as if it would defy any comb or brush. Looking at his stoop shouldered, skinny frame, it was hard to believe that her opponent had been a rail splitter, a shopkeeper, a lawyer, a congressman and the Commander in Chief of the United States of America.

Basketball had not been invented when Abraham Lincoln made the passage from the other side to New Jerusalem. When he first saw it played here, however, it reminded him of how as a boy, he and his sister Sarah used to make a game of tossing cabbages into split oak baskets, while gathering in an Indiana field. He was always physically fit and athletic as a young man, and when he discovered basketball in Heaven, he fell in love with the sport.

Abe was always on the lookout for a quick game of pickup with a worthy opponent, and the tall, blue eyed redhead that he just competed with, proved to be quite a challenger. Kelsie was delighted to discover that her new body and abilities gave her the skill to 'dunk' with ease, and that she could compete with anyone she chose. She and Abe had played for the best two out of three games, to a hundred points, and she had edged him out during the last game. At first, Abe took it easy on her because she was a girl, but he soon found himself fighting to stand his ground. In the end, it had been a fun time, and a unique experience; a basketball tournament between a high school girl and one of the most famous Presidents in American history. This could only happen in New Jerusalem, they were both thinking at the same time.

Abe picked up the ball and turned to Kelsie. "Do you want to make it the best three out five?" he offered.

Kelsie held up her hands and shook her head. "Thanks, but no. I'm gonna take a break." Abe looked a bit dejected. "Hey maybe later, okay? I just want to watch somebody else for a while."

Lincoln brightened. "You know where to find me, Red. It's been fun, but I'm not going to let you win next time," he said with a hint of sarcasm, stepping up to the free throw line and taking a shot.

Kelsie rolled her eyes. "You didn't let me win, this time, Abe. Work on your outside game. You're going to need those three pointers," she said, walking back to the locker room.

Kelsie walked into the locker room, removed the wristband she had been wearing, and turned it in to the attending angel to retrieve her sword. The wristband was actually more like a thick metal bracelet, made of the same transparent steel that their swords were, and inscribed layer upon layer with Scripture. It enabled anyone that was engaged in a sporting event to keep the Word with them, without having to carry their sword. The exception of course, was if someone was competing in fencing. Then the sword came in quite handy.

She looked down at her simple white t-shirt and bright lime green basketball shorts, and thought about changing. Fortunately, she had found that since one didn't perspire in Heaven, bathing was not unnecessary, although one could certainly indulge in a hot shower or a long bath, if they chose. She also found that her clothing could be changed at will just by thinking about it. As she envisioned the transformation, the material of her shirt, shorts and athletic shoes, grew and changed, both in texture and color. Her shirt was now a snap front, western cut affair with piped yokes. Her shorts became boot cut Levi's and her shoes were now cowboy boots, with intricate stitching across each sharp toe. Perfect, she thought. You can take the girl out of the country, but you can't take the country out of the girl.

The angel brought Kelsie's sword to her, and she thanked him, hanging it on her side. "I watched you play," the angel said. "You gave Abraham a run for his money. And I think if he had met you on the other side, you might have gotten a chance to be the First Lady," he joked, as a faint smile touched his expression. He was big, like the other angels she had met. This one had a bronze complexion and long blonde locks, like a California personal trainer on growth hormones. Ironic, Kelsie thought, given the post he was working here in a sports facility.

"Too bad for him then, since we were about a hundred and fifty years out of step with each other. Besides, I was taken," she said, thinking about the curly haired country boy she had walked into Heaven with. I wonder where he is and what's he's doing, she thought. *I guess I find out soon enough. Noah has to check this place out.*

Kelsie had no idea how long she had been at the New Jerusalem Sports Complex, but she was having the time of her life, or afterlife, that is. Her former grandmother, Betty, had stayed with her for a while, but when it became apparent that Kelsie was going to be happy to stay there for some time to come, Betty had left, promising to see her again when she wished. They had embraced in a long hug, and both were elated to know the other was at peace and enjoying the wonders of the paradise God had prepared for them.

Since she had come there, Kelsie had taken in many sporting events, both as a spectator and as a participant. She had played soccer with former World Cup competitors from a dozen countries. She had watched auto races, where vintage looking, open wheeled, Indy style cars, with engines literally powered by thunder and lightning, were driven by the likes of Barney Oldfield and Steve McQueen. She had seen a young black woman from Tennessee named Wilma Rudolph compete against an ancient Greek Olympian named Cassius, and had tried her hand at fencing, javelin throwing, Scottish hurling and now, Presidential basketball.

The New Jerusalem Sports Complex was like a city unto itself, and it would have taken every variant and channel of ESPN's extensive sports network to have covered them all. Some of the most impressive contests even included angels, who enjoyed playing with their human fellow servants. Many times, the sons and daughters of man were somewhat outmatched by the angelic hosts, but there were exceptions. It was said that Jacob, son of Isaac, would gladly wrestle any angel, any time, usually to a draw. Apparently, he had experience in that area of competition.

After stopping by one of the local snack bars, Kelsie sat down on a sleek bench shaped of solid platinum under a spreading birch tree and watched the people pass by. She sipped a tall glass of iced coffee that was flavored with some sort of peppery fruit that she didn't recognize and munched on the best corn dog she had ever eaten. She had no idea how long she had been there. She had lost track of time. She could have spent only hours here; although it felt much more like days, or perhaps as much as a year. *It is so hard to keep up with time here,* Kelsie thought; *I may have been here for a decade.* But she was glad that time wasn't an issue anymore. She hadn't seen a single clock, wristwatch, or even a sundial since she had been there. Time really had no meaning.

That wasn't a bad thing at all, she decided. Like many teens, Kelsie had been challenged to get to school on time, to make practices, games, and other events. Now, none of it mattered. The thing she wondered about though was when it was time to move on. She had enjoyed her time here, but she knew that ultimately, she wanted to be with Noah. She didn't really know how or doing what, but she knew she wanted to share her time in Heaven with him. From what he told her, he wanted the same. She thought, s*o when do I leave here?*

As soon as she considered the question, the answer was self-evident. If she was thinking about leaving, the time to go was now. She didn't know if she would be early or late to meet up with Noah, but somehow, she thought if it was meant to be, she would be right on time. Kelsie got up, looked at her boots and watched them transform into a comfortable pair of lime green canvas high tops. Her jeans transformed into khaki running shorts, and her top became a light blue t-shirt, with iridescent butterfly emblazoned across the front. "It looks like it's time to go," she said to no one but herself, and broke into an easy paced run, down the path, between rows of gyms, coliseums, tracks and playing fields, out the gate, and down the road, to the Rueben Way Gate.

CHAPTER TWENTY TWO

"A re you sure you won't come with me?" Noah asked, as Bud and Dennis stood with him at the gate of the guild. "It's going to be a good time. I've got a good feeling about this."

Bud chuckled and said, "I'm sure you do. This is right up your alley. But we've already been with you to the Builder's Guild, the Art Guild and the Guild of Engineering. We helped you build your little mechanical 'project', for goodness sakes. I need to get back to the ranch. Your Uncle Slim, Cousin Joe and Great Granddad Henry are probably wondering where I am. We've got some horses to break. Besides, I think you'll want to spend more time here anyway," he continued, gesturing toward the guild gate. "You know where I'll be. Just head out the Judah Road Gate, turn left and ask around for the 'Big W' Ranch. You can't miss it."

Dennis nodded in agreement. "Yeah, and I promised your Great Grandpa Cecil that we would build a boat to go fishing. He's going to name it 'Marie' and surprise your great grandmother with a cruise. You've got this, Noah. Go have fun- it's what God made you for."

Noah grinned and nodded. "I love ya'll. You don't know how much. It just makes me happy to know I can see you when I want. My grandfathers . . . now, my brothers. I'll see you soon," he said, hugging them both and kissing them on the cheek.

Dennis and Bud parted ways and left Noah leaning against the 'project' Bud had mentioned. Noah had drawn the concept at the Art Guild, while his companions had assisted him with the machining and assembly at the Engineering Guild. The finished result was impressive.

The motorcycle was a work of highly polished stainless steel and white candy pearl enamel art, with a deep blue lacquer racing stripe running down its center, flecked with tiny sparkling flakes of gold and diamond dust. It sat on gold spoke wheels wrapped in fat white rubber tires, with deep tread, carved into the silhouette of a herd of galloping horses. The engine was unlike anything anyone had ever seen on the other side, designed to be powered by rare earth pistons, driven by the electromagnetic energy of the ball of lightning that could be seen flashing like a welding arc through the observation glass on the side of the tank. With one hundred million volts of power on tap, it would run a thousand years before it needed a fill up. Across each side of the tank, were emblems of capital block letters, made of carbon fiber, outlined in gold. The emblems read:

"WHITE KNIGHT 4.0".

Noah had owned two white motorcycles and one large white Ford F-150, and he had referred to them all as the White Knight. Somehow, he suspected though, this would be the last one.

While some might think that it was ironic of Noah to continue to enjoy motorcycles after he and Kelsie's tragic ordeal, he knew different. With the element of danger taken out of the equation, there was no reason for him not to appreciate a pleasant cruise in Heaven on a good bike. Given his current situation, Noah thought, a leisurely ride on a pretty spring afternoon may have been one of the best things that ever happened to him.

Noah turned from his pet creation and looked beyond the guild gate. He stood in awe of the bell spires, concert halls, and amphitheaters that lay beyond the gate where he stood. He could hear strains of music, from primitive drums, to full classical orchestras coming from the grounds beyond. Styles ranging from jazz, classical, rock, blue grass . . . even reggae could be distinguished, as musicians plied their talent within the Music Guild.

Noah checked his sword to make sure it was secure, strapped lengthwise across the handlebars. Throwing a leg over the hand tooled leather saddle of the White Knight, he touched a pearl button just below the right hand grip and the exhaust pipes literally thundered to life. He popped the bike into gear with the toe of his left boot, and let the bike idle up the drive quietly, so the musicians would not be disturbed as they played.

Noah pulled up in front of a beautiful building with a crystal façade, inlaid with eighth notes, sharps, flats, trebles clefs, and other musical symbols. In front was a statue of David, playing a harp, accompanied by Mozart, seated at a piano forte and Keith Green, strumming a guitar. *What, no drummer?* Noah mused to himself. Below the statue was a sign that read 'WELCOME CENTER'. This was a common layout for most guilds he had seen, giving newcomers a place to come, so they could get an idea of where things were on campus. He parked in the grass out front, dropped the kickstand, strapped on his sword and strolled in.

A few folks were in the lobby. Noah approached a Sudanese girl in a colorful traditional dress and bare feet and asked where he might need to go. "If you have just arrived, you will want to go there," she said, indicating a doorway leading into what appeared to be a large library lined with bookcases. She answered him in her native Bedawi language, and since he had grown so accustomed to his newfound ability of interpretation, Noah didn't even notice. He merely thanked her in flawless Bedawi, and stepped through the doorway.

The room was approximately half the size of a football field, Noah guessed, lined with bookcases that were as high as the fifty foot ceiling. Most of the shelves were filled with nearly identical leather bound volumes. He turned to a shelf at eye level near the door, and read the title printed on the spine of one book. The gold leaf letters read "Amazing Grace, Volume 11,986". The books next to it were identical, except for being Volume 11,987, Volume 11,988, and so on.

Facing him in the center was a large table, with a volume open on it. Behind the table sat an angel, quietly thumbing through another volume, seemly absorbed in the contents. There was a bottle of ink and a basket of old fashioned quill pens sitting on the table to his right. Across the front of the table were engraved the words, "THE LIBRARY OF AMAZING GRACE".

As Noah approached the table, the angel looked up from his reading and greeted him. "Hail, Son of man. You are the one called *Rea' Adam-El Yada' Mela'kah;* Friend of Man and God, Skilled in All."

Noah was taken aback. "Uh, Yeah, I guess that's me, but you can call me Noah, since that's a quite a mouthful. How did you know my given name?"

The angel gave him a sardonic smile and pointed to Noah's chest. "I can read." Noah looked down and saw that his white stone had slipped from beneath his shirt. His cheeks grew hot and flushed bright pink, as he tucked the chain beneath his collar.

"What is this place?" asked Noah. "What are all these books? They all say 'Amazing Grace' on them."

The angel stood slowly, and began a reverent monologue that he had obviously delivered many, possibly millions of times.

"When an alcoholic slave ship captain named John Newton fell so far into the pit of sin, addiction and depravity that he found his sanity slipping away, he turned to the God he had ignored, denied and even cursed. There he found the forgiving power of Christ, as he was gloriously born again and tasted the unfathomable grace of our Father, Jehovah Yahweh. He was so moved, that not only did he devote the balance of his mortal life to ministry, he penned a simple hymn that has become the most powerful Christian anthem ever known, in Heaven and Earth. That hymn is 'Amazing Grace.'

'Amazing Grace' has been sung in virtually every language known to man, with endless variants, set to hundreds of melodies. It is the most popular song of all time. This library is devoted to that hymn. You may have heard as little as one, or as many as a dozen verses to the song during your life, but here, every son or daughter of man that enters may make the song their own, by adding their own verse, telling their own story of the amazing grace that transformed their lives and purchased for them this blessed eternity."

Noah was awestruck at the thought. All these volumes were filled with verses that were added to 'Amazing Grace' by millions of men, women and children that had entered into the eternal bliss of a life in the presence of God. "Incredible," he breathed, looking around. "I cannot wait to hear an angel choir do this," he said, spreading both arms to indicate the contents of the shelves.

The angel simply looked Noah in the eyes and said, "I'm sorry, Son of man, but angels do not sing."

"They don't WHAT?" Noah was a bit incredulous. "But I've heard about angels singing all my life."

"Where have you heard this?" the angel asked rhetorically. "Stories? Songs? Christmas plays? Certainly you have not read it in the Bible, because it is not there. It is a tradition and a fable among the sons and daughters of men. But no, angels do not sing. We have our own means of worship to be sure. But singing is a human characteristic. It is a form of expression, worship and art uniquely reserved for the sons and daughters of men."

Noah looked at the angel with a mixture of emotion. On the one hand, he felt extremely blessed that he had been given such a special gift, taken for granted by so many. On the other, he almost pitied the angel standing before him. This extraordinary creature possessed incredible supernatural power and clearly admired the gift of song; but it was beyond the scope of his ability to raise his voice in even a simple children's chorus of 'Jesus Loves Me.'

If the angel had any feelings other than appreciation for singing, however, he did not show it. He looked at Noah with dark, shining eyes, obviously interested in seeing what Noah might write. "Well, Noah," he said, "Would you like to give it a try?" He held out a quill with one hand and slid the bottle of ink across the table with the other.

Noah took the quill in his hand and studied the blank page before him. He stroked the ball of his thumb across the point of the pen, testing its sharpness, and reached within himself for words that would tell of his own journey. Noah tried to think about the traditional melody of the old hymn, but he kept playing the words in his mind to the minor chords of a classic rock tune…'The House of the Rising Sun'. Not surprising, Noah thought. The melody works perfectly with the meter of 'Amazing Grace'.

He opened his mouth and sung the first verse *acapella*, in those haunting minor strains. The angel listened in rapt attention, as Noah sung:

Amazing Grace, how sweet the sound,
That saved a wretch like me.
I once was lost, but now I'm found.
T'was blind, but now I see.

As he finished the original verse, words of his own welled from the depths of Noah's heart. Without missing a beat, he dipped the pen into the ink, touched the point to the paper, and began to write his own verse, singing as he did so:

The world I left was scarred by sin,
Its love and pain combined.
Now all my pain is washed away,
And all God's love is mine.

As the sound of his voice fell silent, Noah looked at the words on the page, blew gently across them, and watched the ink dry into the paper. He looked up, just as the angel smiled at him and wiped a single tear from his own cheek. "We're not supposed to do that here," the angel said, "But you got me."

Noah grinned, pleased that he touched the angel in such a personal way. He placed the stopper in the ink bottle, handed the quill to angel and said, "Well, that's my story, and I'm sticking to it."

CHAPTER TWENTY THREE

"Tony, I'm having a hard time getting the 'G' chord on this thing," Noah said, as he fumbled with the fingering of the unusual guitar's fret board.

Antonio, a short, swarthy Italian, shook his head and moved Noah's fingers across the strings to a new position. "You have to remember that this instrument is tuned to a chromatic scale. The eight strings go from a low 'E' to a high 'E' by half steps, through an octave. Here," he said, producing a folded sheet of paper from his pocket, "I've made a chord chart for this guitar. It's not complete, but it should get you started."

Noah looked at the chart, shifted his fingers and strummed the strings, producing a rich, distinct tone, unlike any guitar he had ever heard. The different tuning and two additional strings, combined with the exquisite materials and workmanship to create an amazing sound. "This thing is awesome," Noah said. "I don't understand how you get such a full tone from such a narrow body."

"Part of it is the materials," a taller, thinner man explained. "The rosewood and maple from the King's Forest is better and straighter grained than anything you've ever seen on the other side. Part of it is

Tony's design and the shape of the body. It acts as an incredible resonator, much the same as the violins he builds."

"True," Antonio replied, "But Les was able to bring some ideas from his electric guitar work into the mix. His influences helped to make the strings lighter, the frets flatter. The fret board is curved. It made it much easier to add two strings and still be playable," he said, with a satisfied smile.

When Antonio Stradivari began crafting musical instruments in Cremora, Italy during the late 1600's, his masterpiece violins became so sought after, that they became the benchmark for stringed instruments for over three centuries. What is not as well known, however, is that in addition to his "Stradivarius" bowed instruments such as violins and cellos, Stradivari also made guitars and mandolins. What is totally unknown to those outside of Heaven is that Antonio, or 'Tony' Stradivari has continued to hone his skill and design in the New Jerusalem Music Guild for over three hundred and fifty years.

Tony's work was most recently influenced by an American guitar picker and designer named Les Paul that arrived in New Jerusalem in 2009. Tony and Les found in each other a kindred spirit, and began to collaborate on the development of truly extraordinary guitars.

The guitar that Noah held was one such instrument. While it was an acoustic guitar, the body was thin, like an electric model. The finish was dark, almost ebony, with a brilliant orange sunburst in the center. It was incredibly light weight, but felt stronger than steel. Noah felt as if a rock star could have used it to cleave the stack of amplifiers in two. With topaz fret markers and gold tuning hardware, it was truly a work of art, built by two masters born eight generations apart.

Noah turned the guitar in his hands and admired its beauty. Someday, he wanted a guitar like this. It was gorgeous and one of a kind. Perhaps he could build one; he certainly had the time. "That's the coolest guitar I've even seen," he said, offering the instrument back to Stradivari.

Tony held up his hands and shook his head. He looked at the guitar's co-creator, and Les gave him a knowing wink. "You keep it," Stradivari said simply. "Consider it a gift."

Noah was utterly speechless. He stood still, his eyes switching back and forth from the guitar to Tony and Les, whom he had only recently befriended during his tour through the Music Guild. They both beamed at him. "Are you serious? No way! I don't know what to say," Noah finally managed.

"A simple thank you will work," Les replied. "We turn these things out all the time. You'll be doing us a favor by taking it off our hands," he said, speaking about the instrument as if it were a cheap, mass produced knock off from a pawn shop, instead of a priceless, hand built work of art, built and signed by Antonio Stradivari *and* Les Paul.

Noah bowed to them gratefully. "Thank you, my brothers. This is one of the sweetest gifts I've ever received. I will play it with honor," Noah said solemnly, as he folded Tony's handwritten chord chart and slipped it into his pocket.

"We are only simple tradesmen," Stradivari replied. "Musical carpenters. Honor God; He gave us the tools, the materials, the hands and the ability."

Carrying his new guitar, Noah continued on his tour of the Music Guild. He had already sampled a dizzying array of wonder here; he enjoyed a concert by a group of very familiar artists that called themselves the Sun Record Boys, as well as a performance by the New Jerusalem Orchestra of Beethoven and Mullins Third Symphony, a collaborative work between Ludwig Van Beethoven and Rich Mullins.

Noah had also played drums in a jam session with a group of former garage band musicians of no significant renown, when a dark haired kid in black named Johnny sat down with a flat top guitar and led them in an improvised medley of religiously themed secular songs. A few lines of 'Jesus is Just Alright With Me' faded into 'Spirit in the Sky', which in turn gave way to a quick jag of 'Your Own Personal Jesus', finishing the set with the chorus of Creed's 'Higher'. Noah loved every minute of it.

Now, with his Stradivari-Paul slung upon his back, he wandered across the campus in search of another concert to enjoy or jam session to join. He stopped to listen to a trio playing a kalimba, steel drums, and bamboo flute, pumping out a Calypso flavored version of 'Ancient of Days'. He found four chords and strummed along, until the sound of a traditional gospel choir unlike anything the world had ever known reached his ears. He finished his session with the Caribbean trio, gave them a nod and a wave, and strode in the direction of the choir music.

As Noah topped a grassy hillside, he saw a huge alabaster band shell that reminded him of pictures he had seen of the Sydney Opera House. Standing on stage was a great multitude in white robes, accented by a blood red sash. The group was composed of every race known to man, but the overwhelming style influence of the music was obviously Black Gospel.

Standing out front was a young woman with skin the color of milk chocolate and a robe the same shade of red as the sashes the choir wore. She conducted in powerful spasms and convulsions, as her throbbing contralto voice rose above and then joined with the others. Her name was Mahalia Jackson. Accompaniment was provided by a Hammond B3 organ, a sleek black grand piano, and a thumping bass guitar. The percussion section consisted of the clapped hands of every choir member, in perfect time. The band shell reverberated as the choir hit the refrain:

I want to be ready,
I want to be ready,
I want to be ready, Lord,
Walkin' in Jerusalem, just like John.

Then, switching gears, the choir performed a chord modulation and changed keys, modifying the lyrics as they did so:

I'm glad I was ready
I'm glad I was ready
I'm glad I was ready, Lord
I'm walkin' in Jerusalem just like John.

Noah clapped his hands and sang along, dancing a bit as he did so. Okay, Noah thought, this lives up to the traditional expectation of a Heavenly choir. Then, as his eyes scanned the stage, he spotted a couple of faces that were familiar to him.

Tilly and Jessica were in the second row from the top. Decked out in white robes, they were singing at the top of their lungs. As Jessica's eyes met Noah and she glimpsed his grinning countenance, the little girl tugged at Tilly's sleeve. Tilly jumped and waved, before the pair climbed down from the stage to greet him.

Noah was nearly knocked down as Tilly and Jessica pounced on him, throwing their arms around their former traveling companion. "Where have you been?" asked Jessica. "The last time we saw you, you were running toward The Thrones."

Noah grinned sheepishly. Yeah, that I was. I spent a lot of time there, but I've definitely been around," he replied.

The trio of friends found a soft grassy spot on the hillside and sat together, catching up with each other. Noah told them of his travels, and he was happy to hear of Tilly's and Jessica's adventures as well. Since much of Jessica's family was still on the other side, she had chosen to tag along with Tilly. Tilly's husband and son had met them at The Thrones, and shown the pair around New Jerusalem. After several stops, including the Crystal Bridge, they found themselves at the Music Guild, and for now, they were happy to check out the choir.

Noah told them about his brother Benjamin being an Emissary, about meeting his grandfathers, and his time spent building the White Knight. He showed them the guitar he had been given and explained who made it. As he finished his tale, however, there was one thing unresolved between them.

"Have you seen Kelsie?" Noah asked, with obvious anticipation.

Tilly gave him a knowing smile. "I wondered how long it would take you to get around to that tall red headed drink o' water. Sure we've seen her. She was jogging down the street at a pretty good clip. We saw her not far from the entrance to the Music Guild."

"Where was she headed? Did she say?" Noah inquired.

Jessica answered. "She said she was going to meet you, just inside the Reuben Way Gate."

"Really?" Noah said, anxiously. "How long ago was that?"

Tilly shook her head a bit. "You know how it is here, baby. Time doesn't apply. It doesn't seem that long, but it could have been quite a while."

Noah nodded, knowing exactly what she meant. Time didn't just fly here; it literally didn't exist. When he had built the White Knight, he omitted the speedometer for exactly that reason. On the other side, speed was measured by comparing distance and time. Since time meant nothing in Heaven, speed was immeasurable. In Heaven, a person truly came to know Simon Peter's meaning when he wrote, "One day is with the Lord as a thousand years; and a thousand years as one day," (2 Peter 3:8, KJV)

"So what are you going to do?" Jessica asked. "Are you going to meet her?" Jessica had overheard Noah's and Kelsie's plan as they had approached The Thrones.

"Yeah, when I'm done here, I'll leave the Guild and meet her there," Noah replied. Although he hadn't realized it, his right foot had begun to tap unconsciously, signaling a slight impatience on his part. He and Kelsie had agreed to 'do their own thing' for a while, but it sounded as if she was ready to meet and begin the next chapter of life in Heaven together.

Tilly could see the wheels turning behind Noah's eyes. "And when do you think you'll be done here? When are you gonna take off and catch her?" Tilly asked with a grin.

Noah blushed a bit, returned her grin and replied, "Well, funny you should ask. I guess I'm ready right about now."

CHAPTER TWENTY FOUR

K elsie sat at a table near a familiar place, talking with a new friend, while sipping frozen cobbler berry lemonade. She had arrived at the Serbian's food stand a short time ago, and had finished a warm olive and mushroom salad with feta stuffed grape leaves, before her newfound companion had asked if he could sit with her, and struck up a conversation. She had spoken of Noah, their journey here and their plan to meet. She had spoken of family, friends and school on the other side. Kelsie enjoyed the discussion and was fascinated by her new friend and his unique point of view.

She was sharing a meal with an angel, named Mizael. A large figure with long, wavy, platinum blonde tresses and fair, smooth skin, Mizael was almost a stereotype of what one might consider to be a 'classic' example of an angel. Wearing a simple white tunic and a large broad sword, he looked as if he only lacked a large set of feathery white wings and a glowing halo. Only one other thing challenged that traditional image; the distinct New York accent that he spoke with, resulting from a long term assignment as a guardian angel in Yonkers.

"What I don't understand," Mizael said, chewing a bite of spicy gyro, "Is why your high school used a devil as a mascot. And why did they make it blue?"

Kelsie laughed. "The color doesn't mean anything. I don't think so, anyway. As far as the devil part, I think they just wanted a mascot that was mean and powerful."

The angel looked a bit perplexed. "Mean? Sure they're mean. But powerful? Daughter of man, they are some of the weakest beings in Creation. Jehovah Yahweh removed most of their power and all of their weapons when they were thrown out of Heaven. Contrary to films you've seen or books you've read, the only powers they have left are lies and hatred."

"I'm glad you brought that up," Kelsie replied, studying the angel carefully. "Why does the Satan and all his demons hate us so much?"

"They hate your dust," Mizael said simply. "They are jealous of it."

"My dust?" Kelsie was baffled by his response. "What do you mean my dust? I didn't know I had any, and if I did, they could have it."

Mizael smiled ruefully, sopping up the remainder of his gyro's mint yogurt sauce with a scrap of flat bread and stuffing into his mouth. "The dust to which I'm referring is long gone; you left it on the other side. It is the dust your earthly body was made from; the dust that all sons and daughters of man are made from. You see, Jehovah Yahweh spoke everything else into existence. Heaven, Earth, the universe, trees, grass, things that fly, creep and swim; even us- He spoke a few words and it all came into being. He did that with all of Creation except for you and your kind. For mankind, He put His hands into the dirt, touched you, formed you, *made* you. When He was finished, He breathed His own breath into you. Because of that, your kind is unique. The dust was cursed because man believed a lie, but God Himself put on a dusty coat of flesh and blood to redeem you and your kind, and that redemption is unlike anything else in Creation. For that reason, Lucifer and his ilk hold humans in extreme contempt and revel in any opportunity to destroy you or lead you astray. He hates all of you in a profound, tangible way because you have the Blood redemption that will forever be beyond his reach."

Kelsie was lost in thought as she stared into Mizael's ice blue eyes. She had been elated the night she gave her life to Christ. She had called her oldest brother Jeb, and he had driven all the way from Kentucky to share in her joy. As excited as she had been that night, as personally loved as she felt when she knelt before The Thrones, feeling the hands and words of Jesus upon her, she had never grasped the gravity of how unique humanity's role in God's Creation was until Mizael explained it to her. She and her kind had a place in God's heart like nothing else, like no one else in the universe. She considered the white stone she had been given. The engraved stone that hung lightly from the small chain around her neck was not just a precious little trinket given to her by the Father; it was a token of that incredible relationship she had with the Creator of everything.

She tugged the chain from beneath her shirt and holding the stone up, she read the words. The letters were inscribed *Bathesh Chayleb Simchah*, the meaning of which she instinctively knew; *Daughter of Fire and Life, Heart of Joy.* When she thought of that name, it felt truer than her given name from birth. From February of 1993, she had been Kelsie Dawn Trobaugh, but for the Father, she had always been His daughter of fire and life, with a heart abundantly full of joy. That was the name of her inception, the name of her destiny, and the name of her eternity.

"A lot to consider," Mizael said quietly, meeting her gaze. "I know it's the tendency of your kind to get 'lost in the crowd'. But this redemption you've been given; it's unique and it's personal."

Kelsie's expression suddenly changed as a thought struck her. "What about you? What about the angels? Do you envy humans? Do you want what we have?

Mizael erupted in a quick, snorting laugh. "Do you remember what the other side was like? Do you remember the struggles? I have spent many years among your people on the other side. You were blessed; you only had seventeen years of the conflicts, the troubles, the curse. Many of your kind live eighty years or more, in constant conflict and pain. Your relationship with God is faith based, believing in Him whom you have never seen. Our lives are much simpler. We believe because we see, because we know. The curse of sin is not such a strong trap for us. We experience no physical pain, no aging, no death," Mizael said, shaking his head. "No Kelsie, we do not envy you. We help you not only because our Father loves you so much, but because we see how desperate your plight is. Your kind is not just mired in sin; they are crippled by it and addicted to it. It takes Blood redemption to get you out. Without it, even the best of your kind are without hope."

Kelsie nodded; she understood what he was saying. As much as she would have loved to do things like go her prom, walk the line during graduation, and consider college, she knew that for her, this life was so rich, so and full in comparison to the things on the other side. She missed her friends and family, but she was hopeful that she would see them again, and with so much ahead of her, looking back didn't occupy much of her time.

Then Kelsie posed another question to the angel. "I know you say that sin isn't as much of a problem for your people, but it can happen, can't it? I mean, it obviously was a problem for Satan and the demons that followed him. Is there any plan in place for angels? For forgiveness, I mean."

"Yes, and that's one more reason for Satan to hate humans," Mizael replied. "The irony is that our judgment and redemption is tied to you and your kind. When time on the other side is no more, your people will judge our people for our dedication and actions. The apostle Paul spoke of it briefly in his first letter to the Corinthian church, but many of your kind have not thought about the implications. Because Lucifer and his minions were so instrumental in the cursed condition of the other side, they know the sons and daughters of men will never judge them worthy of Heaven. Instead, they are certain that your kind will condemn them to eternal darkness of Gehenna."

"I can't get my head around that," Kelsie said, trying to digest the weighty concepts of humans, angels and judgment. Even with her enhanced understanding, the depths of such topics were difficult to grasp. "How will that work? When will it happen?"

"The circumstances surrounding our judgment are as much a mystery to us as yours is to your people," Mizael replied. "As far as when, no one knows when time on the other side will end except for the Father . . . and He isn't telling. But personally, I think it will be relatively soon. Multiple prophecies are coming to pass. There is too much unrest on the other side. The social and spiritual physics of the cursed world is tearing the other side apart. Just as the physical law of entropy says that molecules fall apart, wood rots and metal corrodes, so does the society of the other side. The sons and daughters of man may be inventing new toys and technologies at a break neck pace, but their world is falling to pieces around them."

"You got that right," Kelsie replied. "The other side is a train wreck, and it's only getting worse. I once thought about how tough it would be to raise children in that world. Now, I don't have to worry about it."

"You have a healthy outlook on all this, Kelsie," Mizael said. "You are obviously a strong, intelligent young woman. I am happy for you. May your friends and family see you soon."

As they fell silent for a moment, the ground beneath their feet trembled faintly. A deep subterranean rumble coming from the center of the city was not so much heard as felt in the bones. A couple of pedestrians stopped and turned, looking down Reuben's Way for the source. As Kelsie and Mizael listened, the rumble grew louder, as if its source grew closer.

"Is that thunder?" Kelsie asked, looking at Mizael with an inquisitive expression. "We don't have rain here, do we?"

"Never," Mizael replied, with a slight tone of uncertainty in his voice. "I don't know what it could be, but there's something about it that sounds vaguely familiar."

"Yeah, it does," Kelsie agreed, trying to focus on the rumble. Then, suddenly a ghost of a smile broke across her face, growing until it became a broad grin. "I know what it is," she said, standing and looking down the thoroughfare.

"Then what is it?" Mizael asked. "Don't keep me in suspense. I know I recognize that tone; I just can't put my finger on it, as your kind says. It's like something from the other side, only different."

"That's because it is something from the other side, only different," Kelsie said. "It's Noah. It's got to be."

As she stood with Mizael watching, a pinpoint in the distance grew as the rumble became louder. The pinpoint became an object, the object became a white motorcycle with a blue stripe; upon the motorcycle was a rider, clad in jeans, boots and a t-shirt. A bright blue arc of electrical ozone flashed from the exhaust pipes. Across the handlebars were strapped a sword and a guitar. The White Knight thundered down the road, slowing as it neared, until Noah clutched the engine, revved the twist grip, and grinned as the engine erupted in a thunderclap. He hit the kill switch, kicked the stand into place, and swung a cowboy boot over the bike. He stood, leaving his sword and guitar on the bike and walked purposefully to Kelsie, giving her a hug and long, sweet kiss. "Hey girl, I've missed you. I hope you haven't been waiting long." Putting left arm around her, he looked up at the big angel standing with her, stuck out his right hand and said, "I'm Noah. Great to meet you."

CHAPTER TWENTY FIVE

For Noah and Kelsie, there were three shared moments of their lives that defined their destiny. The first time was when they met. Kelsie had accompanied her father to work one evening to deliver a Christmas tree for the department her father supervised. While David Trobaugh had walked away from his daughter and his truck, searching for a forklift, Kelsie had met the smiling, curly haired country boy that had stolen her heart. It was apparent that they were both cut from the same cloth, and soon, they had spent every hour they could with each other.

The second moment was on the last day of their mortal lives, when they had met the destiny that surprised everyone in Noah's and Kelsie's life except God. Their lives had been planned and designed to an exact beginning, length, end and purpose. When the time had come, they had left the other side together. While it was not correct to say their work on Earth was finished, it was understood that their mortal life was. The remainder of influence that their testimonies had in the mortal world, which was still quite substantial in their home communities, would have to be completed posthumously.

The third moment that changed everything for them was when Noah rolled up at the Reuben Way gate on the White Knight, picked up

Kelsie, and drove away, waving goodbye to the angel Mizael and the Serbian. The pair rode out the gate, into the countryside and hung a right turn, departing from the gold paved highway and traveling into the hills several miles outside the walls. They rode until they found a place on a ridge, surrounded by fields and trees, with a bubbling creek spilling through the valley below. Cobbler berries, dvash trees and bush beef dotted the landscape. Butterflies and hummingbirds darted and swooped among stands of wildflowers.

Noah killed the motorcycle engine and kicked the stand into place as Kelsie stepped off the back of the bike. He watched her as she walked out onto the brow of the hillside and looked into the valley below. Drinking it in for a long moment, she finally looked at Noah with an excited sparkle in her eyes. "This is the place, isn't it?" she said, with a smile that was even brighter than their surroundings.

Noah looked at her intently, considering where he was and whom he was with. He looked around, slid off the bike, strode to Kelsie, and putting his arms around her, kissed her and held her for what seemed like a long time. He stepped back, put his arm around her shoulder and turned both of them to face the exquisite view. "It's perfect," Noah said with reverent satisfaction. "This is where we can build our eternity."

Noah and Kelsie had determined to live their lives as brother and sister, in perfect harmony and purity, with a love unmarred by the complications of sexual tension, jealousy and financial hardship. This new life was a natural transition for them; Kelsie had enjoyed the protection and masculine companionship of her two brothers on the other side, while Noah had been closer to his sister than virtually anyone else in his life. The desire to engage in physical passion no longer existed for them; and even now, the past carnal urges they had experienced in their young lives were a distant memory. Now, every kiss was pure, every embrace genuine and beautiful. They were like children in a brave new world; children with incredible wisdom, power and life.

The two of them enjoyed quite a bit of exploring before laying the foundations of their new home together on the hills overlooking the stream and the fields below. Kelsie discovered a flat outcropping of bedrock that turned out to be a solid vein of turquoise, and it would work beautifully as the foundation for the house that they would build. Noah had searched the nearby forests and found a dizzying variety of timber to choose from—cherry, oak, teak, sandalwood, popular, chestnut, mahogany, ironwood, ash and a half dozen species never seen by man. Even the dogwoods here grew straight and tall, with a circumference and height like a mighty oak, and snowy blossoms in perpetual bloom.

At first, they considered how they might build without tools. They had both experienced the substance of Heaven yielding to them, but how would they begin such a project? What about cutting trees? Was harvesting timber or stone from the land acceptable? Even if it were, would they want to mar the countryside?

Noah and Kelsie stood before a hickory that reaching skyward for over a hundred feet. Kelsie was awestruck by its majesty. "How can we take something like this that God obviously planted long before our great, great grandparents? These trees are like a legacy landscape in His front yard. I haven't seen a single thing die since we've been here. Even the meat we've eaten is really just a type of fruit. What happens if we cut something like this down?"

Noah noted her concern, and considered what he had learned about the land of Heaven so far. "From what I've seen, this land was made for us; God created it to perpetually provide for our needs. If I'm right, I don't think we'll have to cut it down. I think it will give us what we need and we can leave it where it stands." He ran his hand across the shaggy, rough bark of the hickory, closed his eyes and concentrated. Then, opening his eyes with a purposeful expression, he deftly slipped his thumb beneath one of the long scales of bark running parallel to the hickory's trunk.

Noah's thumb slipped through the woody exterior of the hickory bark and as he slid his thumb upward, the bark opened as easily as if it were fitted with a zipper. The bark yielded to his touch, and as he widened the space he slipped the fingers of both hands into the opening and pulled, parting the bark as one might open a set of drapes. A long section of green log was exposed, its grain clearly visible. "Very cool," Noah breathed, half to himself. He chanced a glance at Kelsie, and seeing the wonder in her eyes, he smiled with newfound confidence. "Watch this," he said.

Noah plunged his fingertips into the wood, and surprisingly, it gave to his touch. His fingers sunk deep into the log itself. It wasn't that the wood was soft and weak; it was just that Noah's hand was able to pierce the green hickory without the slightest effort. He dug his other hand into the wood and pulled, peeling a large beam of green hickory out of the living log. He pulled until the length of lumber was perhaps twenty feet in length and twisted it suddenly, snapping it free and separating it from the tree. Noah then laid the wood on the ground, and turning back to the tree, he tugged the bark back together. As he smoothed the surface with his hands, he watched as the tree knit back together beneath his touch, without so much as a scar in the bark. When he was finished, neither he nor Kelsie could discern that the tree had ever been harmed, yet it had yielded a beam that was twenty feet long and perhaps ten inches square.

"That is amazing," Kelsie said, placing a hand on the tree in the spot where Noah had opened the bark. "How did you do that? How did you even know that you could do that?" Her blue eyes were full of a mixture of inquiry and awakening revelation.

"To be honest, it was just a hunch, although I have seen similar work before," Noah replied. "The men that made my guitar, the ones that helped me build the White Knight; none of them used tools. They shaped things with their hands. If you remember, we did it ourselves when we first got here. As we climbed down the mountain, the rock literally gave to our touch."

"I remember that!" Kelsie exclaimed. "It was a weird sensation; almost as if the rock turned to clay, then back into rock after it had molded into a hand hold. But how? How do we have this ability?"

"It's who we are, Kelsie," Noah stated simply. "We are created in God's image. He is able to shape the materials of reality to His will. When He made us, God didn't make us to look like Him; He made us to *be* like Him. God made us to create, to have the authority to create. I suspect that we are no different than Adam was before he and Eve sinned. God gave them dominion and power over the animals, the earth, everything. It was theirs to use and care for. But they didn't even break a sweat until after they were thrown out of Eden, after the death of sin." He picked up the beam of green hickory as if it were made of

Styrofoam, even though it weighed several hundred pounds. "We have the ability to do what we want and God has given us the resources to do it with. The only limits we have are the ones we learned on the other side . . . and I'm forgetting those fast."

Kelsie took hold of the free end of the beam and ran her hand across it, squaring the end and shaping the surface to a satin smooth finish with merely her touch. "Well then," she said, flashing Noah a broad grin. "Let's just see what we can do. Let's build ourselves a house."

CHAPTER TWENTY SIX

T he house was a two story log and timber frame structure that was as much a work of art as is was a home. The finishes were fine and natural, with a soft satin sheen on all the surfaces, letting the wood grain of even exterior walls show through with depth and detail. No nails, screws or pegs were used; the wood was simply fused together.

Timber that would have been indigenous to Kelsie and Noah's Tennessee birthplace, such as popular, oak and hickory, were used along with exotic woods like cocobolo, grenadilla, teak and ironwood. Lumber that would have been reserved for fine furniture, such as cherry, maple and walnut were used for floors and paneling. Chestnut, virtually extinct on the other side, was readily available and used by the pair to craft a set of eight chairs and a beautiful matching table.

A broad, winding staircase to the second level was crafted from single piece mahogany, extruded and shaped by Kelsie, with her bare hands and force of will. It was an amazing accomplishment, and after the staircase was finished Kelsie looked at it in wonder, as if someone else had done it. Noah made the ridge beam from a single timber of dogwood, appreciating the irony of using a tree that was cursed with a weak, spindly body on the other side. Tradition held that it had been the wood used for the Cross, and had been cursed by God for that reason, although Noah did not know if that were actually true. Given that supposed history however, he smiled at the thought of using a dogwood timber as the focal point of the roof super structure.

Windows and skylights were everywhere, although they stood open, without glass or shutters. No cold, rain or intruder would ever threaten to invade their home; thus, there was no reason for coverings of any kind. Instead, breeze, light, the fragrance of flowers and an occasional butterfly could waft through the house any time. Likewise, the aroma of an occasional home cooked meal easily spilled into the great outdoors, inviting anyone that happened to be outside, to come into the home that Kelsie and Noah made with their own hands.

The center of the house was a huge great room, with comfortable seating around a circular fireplace built of turquoise, agate, onyx and amethyst. It burned coal as dense as black diamonds that stuck out of the surrounding hills in long, ebony veins. The walls were hung with tapestries and artwork, either done by Noah and Kelsie themselves, or by neighbors that stopped by occasionally with gifts and conversation. It was a warm and inviting place; the pair found themselves more at home there than any placed they had ever lived.

They gathered bush beef, cobbler berries, and various fruits from the hillsides, constantly discovering new bounties of the land. Kelsie discovered a root vegetable that grew along the edge of the stream, with a flavor and texture similar to lobster, much to her delight. Noah rounded up a few goats out of the hills that seemed content to stick around for the company and the grazing. They provided rich, flavorful milk, butter and cheese. Kelsie taught herself to cook, making use of the abundant food and herbs that surrounded them. They became proficient homesteaders on the frontier of Heaven.

Visitors were fairly frequent. Newcomers into the land would often roam across the countryside, on their way to New Jerusalem, and stop for a little hospitality. All ages, races, and backgrounds continued to pour into the land, bringing stories, traditions and news from the other side. As the travelers rested with them, Noah would often break out his guitar and play a few tunes, learning new ones from other regions and peoples as they chatted, while Kelsie would often amaze guests with her developing culinary skills.

Children were a special treat to the pair. Since Noah and Kelsie left the other side as teens, they retained a love for play and fun. The war torn streets and famine ravaged villages of the other side may have been a dusty place of sorrow and tears, but those places of destruction and desolation in Third World countries provided Noah and Kelsie with an unending supply of fresh faced children to run and climb trees with.

During one of their frequent forays into the surrounding countryside, they had discovered a small herd of wild horses, giving Noah an idea. Even though he and Kelsie still sometimes fired up the White Knight and went thundering through the countryside, somehow the notion of being on horseback better suited their new lives. With a little coaxing, Noah had managed to get a palomino mare and a buckskin stallion to follow him home. After a couple of spirited rounds of 'getting acquainted', the horses settled down and consented to be ridden by Noah and Kelsie.

Noah named his buckskin "Dusty", while Kelsie referred to her palomino as "Maggie", after a friend of hers from the other side. They rode the beautiful animals for miles at a time, exploring the countryside, visiting neighbors, and making occasional trips into the city. They traded in New Jerusalem, made friends, but always returned home to their hillside mansion of timber and stone. The two of them had become accustomed to living their bucolic lifestyle in the countryside of Heaven.

Time passed without meaning. It was morning when it felt like morning; afternoon was the ghost of an impression, rather than a time measured by sun or clock. Night never came, never hinted at coming. They napped when they felt like it, just for the sheer simple pleasure of it, rather than a need for it. They never tired; they never got sore or fatigued. Their energy abounded; their physical, spiritual and emotional strength increased steadily. Every moment, they experienced something new; every moment, Heaven became more real. The former life seemed like a dream.

Kelsie finished plating a platter of crispy fried pies stuffed with a variety of both sweet and savory fillings. She placed the platter on the table and walked to the doorway of their house to call Noah in for a meal. She gazed at him as he sat on a solid chuck of pale pink quartz and stared off into the distance, almost in a trance.

Noah's thick wooly hair now tumbled nearly to his shoulders, while his beard had filled in, giving him the appearance of a prophet in faded jeans, cowboy boots and a white t-shirt. His elbows rested upon his knees and his sword lay unsheathed across his open palms. As she looked at the flat turquoise outcropping that stretched for several feet beyond, she could see words that were projected on the stone as light filtered through the layers of the sword's transparent blade.

Also I heard the voice of the Lord, saying, Whom shall I send, and who will go for us? Then said I, Here [am] I; send me. (Isaiah 6:8, KJV)

Kelsie sensed that he was absorbed by concentration. He didn't notice her presence, as he normally did when she approached. "What are you thinking about?" she asked, strolling up behind him and putting her hands on his shoulders.

"Just all of this," he said quietly. "If you had told me on March 19, 2010, that I would be here, now, with you, I wouldn't have believed it. If you had told me that we would live our lives together in a mansion built with our own hands, in a paradise like this, I couldn't have got my head around it. But here we are, doing what we want, when we want, with virtually no limits to our lives. It is awesome. It's more than awesome; it's beyond comprehension."

Kelsie picked up on a note in his voice. "Why do I feel like there is a 'but' coming up somewhere? Are you happy, Noah? Is this what you want? Do you want to be with me?" She stepped into his line of sight so she could study his face.

He looked at her and smiled, putting his hand on hers. "You know I do," Noah replied. "It's just that I guess I'm getting a bit restless. I love this place and I love you, but you and I are both built for adventure, you know? I love to play and I love to work, and I love to be doing something."

"Me too," Kelsie replied. "I mean, building this house has been fantastic and I love doing things for you and when you do things for me." She stopped for a moment and considered the ring that she wore on the middle finger of her right hand. Noah had carved it from a single diamond, and it was exquisite. "But I need a little excitement now and then. I mean, hey, I've played basketball with Abraham

Lincoln. You've played drums with Johnny Cash. We've met people from all over the world, all over history, but now we've kind settled down. I wonder if that's what God has in store for us."

"Somehow I doubt it," Noah said. "I want to do something for Him, and I think we'll get the chance. I feel . . . called to do something. I'm just a little impatient, I guess. But you know, when we were meant to find each other, we did; on the other side and in New Jerusalem. They say God is never late and He's never early; He's always on time." He stood and gave her a little grin. "I just wish He would hurry up and be on time," he said, jokingly.

"You may want to be careful of what you wish for, Noah," a familiar child's voice from behind them replied, startling both of them. They turned and although Kelsie had never met him, she knew who their visitor was. He had same curly brown hair, big brown eyes like his sister and the simple white robe of an Emissary. It was Benjamin, Noah's brother, standing between them and the house. "I'm glad to see you brother, and it's a pleasure to meet you Kelsie. I love what you both have done with this place. But as you might guess, this isn't a social visit. I've come as an Emissary for Jehovah Yahweh. The Father has need of your service."

CHAPTER TWENTY SEVEN

K elsie watched Benjamin as he and Noah chewed through the plate of fried pies sitting before them. She saw so much of Noah in him; not just the tangle of curls, but the blush of his ruddy cheeks, the freckles that peppered his nose. Some of his mannerisms were even reminiscent of Noah; the way he cocked an eyebrow in mock seriousness, way he laughed. There was no denying it. Even though they had not been raised together, the bloodline was obvious.

"These are great," Benjamin said. "What's in this?" he asked, indicating the rapidly disappearing meat pie in his hand.

"Bush beef, onions, goat cheese and something like basil we found growing in a clearing near here," Kelsie replied, pleased at the compliment. "I'm glad you like them, Ben. Can I call you Ben?"

The boy peered at the tall red head with a shy smile. "Certainly," he replied. "No one ever has, but I like it. It's what you call a 'nickname', right?"

"Yeah, I guess that's what you call it," Noah said. "It's a pretty common practice on the other side. Nicknames are either a shortened version of your given name, or sometimes based on some kind of characteristic you have. Sometimes they're nice; sometimes they're not."

Benjamin turned to his brother and asked, "What is the short version of your name?" He looked genuinely curious.

Noah laughed. "I guess Noah is short enough. Some guys used to call me 'Willy', but that was just on the baseball team."

The answer only brought another question to Ben's mind. "What is baseball?"

Kelsie looked at him wide eyed, then at Noah. "Oh, Ben," she said, "You got to get out more. We need to teach you a few things; it sounds like a trip to the Sports Complex is in order."

"I would like that," Benjamin replied, "But there will be plenty of time for that later. Right now, there's work to be done."

"Yeah, about that," Noah said, "I was wondering when you'd get around to telling us why you're here. I mean, don't get me wrong, bro, I'm glad you're here, but as they say, you're 'on a mission from God' right?" He did that last part in his best John Belushi/Jake Blues impersonation.

Benjamin met Noah's laughing eyes with a blank stare; the joke was obviously lost on him. "I don't know who 'they' are, but you're right, I am on a mission from God. He wants both of you to join with an expedition to the King's Canyon. He has need of you there."

Kelsie repeated the name. "King's Canyon . . . sounds very cool; kind of 'western' like."

Benjamin gave her the same blank look he had given Noah. "Actually, it is north of the city. It is a large canyon, reserved for the King's use."

"Large, huh? Would you say it's a 'Grand' canyon?" Noah quipped, with a sneering cocked eyebrow and a wink to Kelsie.

"Oh, quit it!" Kelsie said with a grin, before a mystified Benjamin could reply. "We got to stop that," she said, turning to Benjamin in explanation. "Ben, the Grand Canyon is a place on the other side. It's a huge place in the Western United States. That's where the 'western' comment came from. But if everything else I've seen here is any indication, I imagine the King's Canyon makes the Grand Canyon look like a mud puddle."

Benjamin regained his composure. "Thanks for clearing that up," he said, shooting a glance at Noah. "I was lost for a moment. As you've probably figured out, I know little about the other side. As I was saying, you will meet with an expedition to go to the King's Canyon. There, Jehovah Yahweh has his horses pastured. It will be your group's task to round them up."

"So it *is* like a 'western' thing; a trail drive no less!" Kelsie exclaimed.

Noah smiled at the little girl excitement in her eyes. Then he turned to his brother again. "How many horses?" he asked, studying Benjamin's face.

"All of them," Benjamin replied.

"What I mean is, what kind of numbers are we talking? A thousand? Ten thousand?"

"More than you can imagine," Benjamin said. "Only God knows, but it is in the many millions. This is a significant event, as I'm sure you can surmise."

Noah was silent for a moment, considering the task and the possible implications. He wasn't sure why the Father would want the horses rounded up, but he had a pretty good guess. Right now, he had more pressing questions. "How many in our expedition? Where do we meet?"

"There are twelve of you from each region of Heaven. As you may know, your place sits just inside the Rueben region, then the Judah region is just north of here; there are twelve regions in all. With twelve from each region, that's one hundred and forty four total." Noah looked at him, his eyes narrowing with sudden recognition. "I know what you're thinking, Noah," Benjamin said, holding up a hand.

"While the Father likes to work with these kinds of numbers, this group isn't . . . specifically noted in Scripture. He just called this group to perform this task. I know it doesn't seem like a big group, but you've been selected because you can handle the job. You are all to meet at the Levi Road Gate, north of the city. From there, you will travel into the mountains to the King's Canyon."

"What will we do when we round them up?" Kelsie asked. "We can't exactly drive them into the city."

"That's not exactly true," Benjamin replied. "There are stables built for this purpose on the north side, inside the city walls. You will bring them through the Levi's Highway Gate and stable them there."

"One more question," Noah stated, looking his brother in the eye. "Why us? Why are we a part of this mission? I mean, it sounds great, but what have we got to offer?"

Benjamin smiled. "There are three reasons. First, you both have a sense of adventure; this task requires a certain adventuresome spirit. Second, the Father is aware that you both have embraced the abilities given to you here, in Heaven. You understand how few limits there are on your life. You've become builders, accomplished riders and anything else that you need to be. It takes most people a long time to become acclimated to this land; you both have learned very quickly.

Finally, you are willing. You are anxious to serve, and the Father wants to give you that opportunity. So . . . are you in?"

Kelsie and Noah looked at each with a gleam in their eyes. "You know we are," Kelsie replied. "When do we start?"

"As soon as possible," Benjamin said. "If you wouldn't mind putting together whatever provisions you want to take, I'll help Noah saddle the horses."

Noah looked at him. "Are you coming with us?"

Benjamin looked up at his brother. "I will go with you as far as the Levi's Highway Gate, if you will have me."

"I'd love for you to come, Ben. I love you, Bro," Noah said, putting his arm around Benjamin and kissing him on the forehead. Benjamin looked up at Noah and grinned as Noah ran his hand through Benjamin's hair. Although Benjamin was actually older than Noah, their appearance made the roles almost seem reversed.

"That sounds great guys," Kelsie said. "But we only have two horses, and I can't imagine taking the White Knight on this trip. Are we going to take the time to go into the hills and find another one?"

"I'll ride double with Noah until we get a little farther on the way, if that's all right. We have to stop in the Judah Region and get a couple of riders on the way, and I think I can pick up a horse there," Benjamin said.

"Where are we stopping?" Noah asked, considering the area and the task at hand. "We wouldn't be picking up a couple more Tennessee boys would we?"

Now it was Benjamin's turn to give Noah a teasing wink. "Well, your ability in the saddle is a family trait . . . and the Father picked them specifically, just as he selected you. But to answer your question, we'll be stopping at the Big W Ranch."

Kelsie looked at Noah. "Is that your grandfather's place?"

"Yeah," Noah replied. "Bud, and his brother, Slim. I've heard lots about Slim, I just never got to meet him. He passed over before I was born. But I know both of them are some of the best horsemen around. Looks like this isn't just going to be a trail drive. It's going to be a family business venture."

CHAPTER TWENTY EIGHT

Slim Wilson was a real, bonafide cowboy. From the top of his white straw Stetson to the sharp toes of his finely tooled leather boots, his whip thin frame, bronze skin, and bowlegged gait were more genuine than the Marlboro Man. Although he grew up in Tennessee, he looked as if he had stepped out of a cattle drive in the middle of central Texas. He rode horses and traded cattle virtually all his life, and embraced the appearance and lifestyle that was a result.

Over his lifetime, he was involved in stock sales, horse shows and rodeos. He learned to rope and trick ride with the best, and even performed in a traveling rodeo show during the 1960's. One of his favorite tricks included throwing a marble into the air, drawing a six shooter from his hip and blasting it into powder. Although the effect was helped considerably by loading the pistol with shot shells, it was still an impressive display of showmanship and eye hand coordination.

On the other side, he had lived life hard, only slowing down after cancer had taken him out of the saddle. His sins were many and varied, but fortunately for Slim, God's grace was greater. He gave his life to Christ and spent his final months on the other side trying to make amends as best he could.

On the last day of his mortal life, his older brother Bud had shaved and bathed him. Slim ran his hand across his smooth cheek, and said with a hollow, tired smile, "Well, Bud, I guess you've got me ready to bury."

His brother put on a brave face. "No, Slim. You're going to get better. God's going to heal you."

Slim took Bud by the hand and shook his head slowly. "No, he's not, Buddy. God knows I'm weak, and if He lets me get out of this bed, He knows I'll just mess it up again. He's going to take me home." That afternoon, as Bud held his hand, the only prophecy Slim ever spoke came true. He was forty nine years old.

Now, he sat on the broad back of a brown and white spotted mustang filly that was nearly the size of an Arabian and almost twice as strong. His fist was cinched into the surcingle rig of braided line fastened around the horse's chest. When he glanced at Bud, standing on the first rung of the chute, he had a determined gleam in his eye and a clenched tight grin.

"You think you can stay on this big girl until she settles down this time?" Bud asked, with a bit of a challenge in his voice. "She barely cleared the chute last time before your backside hit the ground."

"I can do it, Buddy. Don't you worry your little head about it. She just caught me by surprise, that's all."

"So you thought she was just going to slip out of there and break into a canter, pretty as you please, huh?" another voice drawled in a friendly taunt. Joe Wilson, Slim's oldest son, stood ready to open the gate. He had joined his father and his uncle in 2006, at the age of fifty six, after his own bout with cancer. Since he had grown up a cattleman, when crossed over, he was happy to join up with them, and had enjoyed his time in the foothills of Heaven. While he was a bigger man than Slim and Bud, with lighter skin and hair than either of them, he had inherited his father's eyes, as well as his mischievous sense of humor.

Slim shot him a stern look. "When I get through with her, she'll trot, rack, canter, gallop or amble . . . backwards. Just give me a three count and open the gate." He pulled himself deeper into a rider stance and gripped the mustang's sides firmly with his legs.

"Hang on then," Joe said, stepping back. "Three . . . two . . . ONE!" he shouted, pulling the rope that lifted the lever on the gate. The mustang bolted out of the chute and instantly leapt into the air, clearing the top rails of the corral with all four hooves. She came down hard, spraying dust and fine gravel in a thick cloud and launched again, forward and vertically at the same time. Slim held on this time, not daring to kick his heels into the animal's flanks. This was not a competition; he was attempting to break the horse for riding.

The filly turned her head and twisted into the grip of his hand, loosening the rig around her chest. Slim pulled hard to take up the slack, but he began to slide.

"Hold tight! Don't lose her!" Bud cried, laughing in a deep, loud chuckle. "Lean back and put your weight on her haunches!"

Slim was doing all that Bud directed and more, but it was not enough. The horse began to circle tightly, spinning Slim off balance with centrifugal force. Then, just as he almost regained his control, she dug in her hooves, stopped and twisted her entire body in the opposite direction. The result spun Slim off the horse's back, pinwheeled him into the air, and he landed with a thud, twenty feet from her in the soft dirt. He rolled onto his back and took a deep breath. "I'm glad that doesn't hurt anymore, but I still feel like I broke something."

"Probably just your pride," Joe said sarcastically, strolling across the lot toward Slim and picking up his hat as he did so. It had departed Slim's head long before Slim had departed from his mount. Joe tapped the dust off the brim of the Stetson and offered a hand to his father. "Wanna go three for three?" he asked, as Slim took his extended hand and sprang to his feet. On the other side, a mishap that bad would have landed him in the hospital . . . or worse.

"I think I'll let her take a little break and get her wind," Slim replied, dusting off the seat of his jeans with both hands. "Wouldn't want to wear her out before we got her broke, would we?"

Joe and Bud exchanged knowing looks and nodded at the conspiracy to reserve Slim's pride. "Maybe I'll take a run at her after a while," Bud said. "If you aren't afraid I'll wear her out, that is."

Bud looked at his brother, expecting an equally snappy comeback, but Slim was standing still, his attention fixed. The horse had trotted off onto the opposite side of the lot and was nibbling at a few stray honeysuckle vines that were growing through the rails of the corral. But Slim was looking past the mustang, into the distance. Just as Bud opened his mouth to ask what he was looking at, Slim said, "Looks like we got company."

Bud and Joe turned to the horizon Slim was facing. In the distance, two horses approached. One was a big buckskin stallion, standing perhaps eighteen hands high, carrying two riders. The lead rider wore a red western bib style shirt, with black piping and sleeves that buttoned with gold buttons the length of his forearms. His jeans were faded and comfortable, the same color blue as his eyes, and tucked into the tops of tooled calfskin boots almost the same shade as the horse. He had cut his hair short and shaved his beard for the trip, leaving only a neat mustache, not much larger than Bud's. The straps of a sword sheath and a guitar crossed his chest like ammunition bandoliers, with the instrument and weapon slung across his back. His expression was one of cool, persistent determination. Sitting tall in the saddle, Noah appeared ready to ride anywhere God would ask him to go.

His passenger had the same curly hair as Noah's, and eyes the color of black coffee. With his brother's encouragement, Benjamin had gotten into the spirit of the ride, exchanging his simple white robe for jeans and a tan, open collared tunic, draped with a serape woven in a dazzling array of colors. His feet were shod with moccasins, and with the rest of his outfit and his complexion, gave him the appearance of a boy from the Mexican frontier. He was holding tightly to Noah's waist with both hands, grinning from ear to ear.

The other horse was a palomino, nearly as large as the buckskin, carrying a lone rider. The rider's knee length, red hair was folded into a single, thick braid that flowed across one shoulder and past her waist, resting on the saddle, bound at the end with a gold filigree clasp. She was dressed in a blue broadcloth shirt with a sweetheart neckline, with the fine gold chain that held her white stone shining on her skin of her neck. Her eyes were the shade of the sky on a clear winter's day; a blue of depth and clarity that would make the Pacific envious. She wore simple khaki jeans and chocolate colored riding boots. Her sword hung from her saddle horn, along with a leather bag for supplies. Although Heaven had no sun, her skin was tan and her smile was brilliant. In all, Kelsie sat in the saddle like a queen; Esther, Sheba or Helen, made all the more beautiful by her open, friendly expression and confident demeanor.

Joe let a long low whistle escape from between his teeth. "Bud, I ain't seen that boy since he was maybe fourteen, but he did good, didn't he? I mean, that's some kinda girl. And who's the other one? I don't know him, but looks like a Wilson to me."

"That's Benjamin, Noah's brother," Bud said, answering Joe's last question first. "He's an Emissary—never lived on the other side. That's the reason you haven't seen him before. In fact, I don't know if I've ever seen an Emissary outside the city. As far as Kelsie goes, I've never met her, but Noah told me all about her. But I'd have to agree with you. She is something else; everything Noah said and more. That boy must have had some kind of game," he said with a grin.

"Well of course he did," Slim said slapping Bud on the shoulder. "I'd say it's a family trait. Evidently, he's still the charmer. She's still with him isn't she?"

Bud smiled wanly. "You know it's not like that. Not here. They're more like brothers and sisters now. But I'm glad they're together. I'm happy for them both; they really love one another. You can tell it by the way they look at each other."

Slim returned the smile. "Yeah, from the looks of them, I'd say you're right. They are some good looking kids. Now come on; let's meet these grandchildren of yours."

CHAPTER TWENTY NINE

"Homesick," Noah said, as he carefully spread fresh butter on half of a steaming homemade biscuit and reaching for the strawberry preserves. "That's about the best way I know to describe it. You know, we spent our whole lives on the other side, just knowing that something wasn't quite right, that we just didn't fit, and as soon as we got here, I knew why. It was because I had spent my whole life away from *home*."

Those seated around the table nodded in agreement. "Like a wayfaring stranger, as the song goes," Bud replied. "We were just passing through. But you're home now, Chief. You and this biscuit making beauty of yours," he said, with a chuckle and a wink toward Kelsie. "Kelsie, these are some of the best biscuits I've had in a long time. Did you do this on the other side, or did you pick up this skill here?"

Kelsie blushed. "I wasn't much of a biscuit making girl on the other side. But it's just like I just sorta know how to do what I want to do . . . and I love cooking for Noah and I, just like he enjoys making things for us. That's what I love about Heaven; anything we want to do, we can do. We have the ability and the material to use."

"Which reminds me, Noah," Slim said, savoring the flavors and company of breakfast, "Bud tells me you built quite a motorcycle. I'd kinda like to see that. Where is it?"

"I left it at the house," Noah replied. "It's a beauty, but I didn't think that it would fit with what we are doing right now. I'll bring it by some time, or you can come by our place and see it. It's not going anywhere; I don't think we have to worry about anyone stealing it," he added with a wry smile.

The six of them enjoyed a long meal together, savoring the tastes and company of a good breakfast with family. Slim, Bud and Joe regaled the table with stories of life since they had been in Heaven, as well as on the other side. Noah caught them up on the most current events he could remember, and Kelsie charmed the gathering of country boys with her open, friendly demeanor. On the other side, it had been said of Kelsie that 'she had never met a stranger'. Here, that really was true, since they were all now truly brothers and sisters.

Benjamin was silently transfixed by this reunion with his colorful and talkative relatives, speaking in terms and about experiences that seemed unclear at times. Life had been a mixture of good and bad for all of them, but this time together represented the best of what they had experienced on the other side, as well as in Heaven. Free from the angst and drama of personal problems, jealousy and strife, a family gathering could be one of the sweetest things ever. As much as he enjoyed living in the Father's presence as an Emissary, he reveled in this . . . this . . . love. In spite of all the streets of gold, diamond and ruby encrusted towers, and majestic landscapes of Heaven, one of the most beautiful, most precious jewels that God offered man was this; a simple, joyous family reunion.

They all listened as Noah broke out his guitar and started playing a few tunes. When he started a bluesy version of "Just Build My Mansion Next Door to Jesus", similar to the way he had learned it from his dad, Bud jumped up and began to sing in animated, booming baritone, tapping his foot and waving his hands. As Noah watched, he realized, *this isn't my father's rendition of this song- it's my grandfather's. My dad just learned it from his dad.*

As Noah bent the strings of his guitar into smoky chords of music, Bud gyrated a bit, rolling his eyes, and pointing at Benjamin and Kelsie. He successfully got a grin out of both of them as he growled in a deep voice:

Just build by man-sion,
Next door to Je-sus,
And tell the angels I'm comin' home.
It does not matter who lives around me,
Just so my mansion, sits near the Throne.

As Bud and Noah finished, the group clapped, whistled and laughed. They enjoyed a few more songs and stories, until things began to wind down, giving Joe an opportunity to bring up the mission Benjamin, Noah and Kelsie had mentioned when they first arrived.

"So, what's the deal with this trail drive to King's Canyon?" he asked, resting his gaze on Benjamin. Joe had pale blue, translucent eyes, almost like an Alaskan Husky. It added an air of intensity to his otherwise placid expression that could be a bit unsettling at times.

Something seemed to click deep within in Benjamin, as his mind and spirit recalled the task at hand. "Jehovah Yahweh has personally requested your help gathering His horses from the King's Canyon. There will be one hundred and forty four riders to bring the herd from the Canyon to His stables at New Jerusalem. You all have been called to be five of them."

"That's a lot of horses," Slim commented, sipping a cold glass of milk. "Why is God bringing all of them together? He has been pretty much content to let them roam free. I can't imagine why He would want to stable them."

"He has not told me," Benjamin replied. "The Father has only told me that He has need of them; and that He has need of you," he added solemnly.

"I've got some ideas about the why," Noah said, as he and Kelsie's eyes met with a knowing glance, "But I'll keep my conjecture to myself. If I've learned anything, it's that it doesn't matter why. When God says He needs you, that's enough."

"Agreed," Joe said, as the rest nodded. "I think we all know that; but it doesn't keep us from wondering sometimes, even in Heaven. A hundred and forty four riders, huh? Sounds like a light crew for such a big job. I take it you've got some heavy hitters for this," he said, phrasing it more like a question than a statement.

Benjamin smiled. "Right now there are Emissaries delivering the message to riders throughout Heaven. Many of them have settled in the countryside, like you. You will be working with horsemen from the Mongolian Steppes, ancient Rome, Greece, Persia, and the American West, to name a few. You will be teaming up with soldiers, rodeo cowboys and jockeys; men and women that know horses and know how to work with them."

An air of excitement swept through the group as they considered the idea and the honor of being included in such an elite group. "Any chance that John Wayne would be in the bunch?" Bud inquired, half-jokingly.

"Actually, John Wayne lives in the city, near the Art Guild. He has taken up painting," Benjamin replied. "He's very good at it too. But I think there is an actor in group, as well as an American president."

"Don't tell me, Teddy Roosevelt," Bud said.

"Ronald Reagan," Joe offered a guess. "That would be an actor *and* a president."

Benjamin just looked at them and shook his head. "I'm sorry, I'm not familiar with a lot of the names. Does Jackson ring a bell?" he asked.

"It sure does," Noah replied with a grin. "Old Hickory. How about that? Another Tennessean makes the cut. This is going to be a fun trip."

"Well, let's not sit around flappin' our gums then," Slim drawled, clapping Joe on the shoulder and looking at Bud with a crooked smile. "The Good Lord has need of us and I ain't never been to the King's Canyon. Let's saddle up and ride."

CHAPTER THIRTY

As the group rode away from the ranch, Noah cast a backward glance at the corrals, the barns and the long, low ranch house with the clapboard siding and wrap around porch. Several oak rocking chairs still swayed softly in the breeze, almost as if they invited the group to return as soon as possible. It still seemed a bit odd just to leave a home like that, just as it did when he and Kelsie had left theirs to begin this journey.

There were no locks on the doors, and the homes were left full of furniture and personal possessions. But since they were in Heaven, there was no worry about burglary. The temptation of sin no longer mattered and since everyone had all they needed or wanted, even theft due to need or hunger would never be an issue. Plus, with paving bricks of gold and mountains made of jewels, things that glittered were just that. In Heaven, the most precious things were relationships; with God and His people.

Likewise, a group such as this would have normally had to pack food and provisions; however, every one of them could change the appearance of their clothing by sheer will. They ate and drank for the sheer pleasure of the experience, since their spiritual bodies actually required no real sustenance. When they wanted to eat, food grew abundantly everywhere, in a dazzling variety. Therefore, they took what they wanted and nothing else. They could live off the land, and the land gave of its treasures freely.

As the group rode northward, they were constantly aware of the wall of the city on their distant right; it dominated the landscape. But as they rode through the hills and valleys between the city and the mountain range that formed the perimeter of Heaven, they watched the environment change as they passed from one region to another. The deciduous forests and glades that had been so familiar to them began to give way to areas that seemed like African grasslands. Large expanses of savanna lay before them, with herds of zebra, wildebeest, and impala grazing on a thick carpet of bermuda and elephant grasses. A large pride of lions, watched placidly and contentedly from the shade of a grove of acacia trees, disinterested in the potential buffet of prey before them.

"It's not a 'lion laying down with the lamb' moment," Kelsie remarked with a grin, as she pointed at the big cats, "But it will do."

Noah looked at Benjamin, who was riding along on a bay pony with white rear 'stockings' from Bud and Slim's ranch. "Are there a lot of different regions like this? I mean, different climates, like on the other side."

"Virtually every biome you would see on the other side it present here, as well as others that are unlike anything on the other side," Benjamin replied. "There are hardwood forests like the one where you live, wetlands, tropical rainforests, jungles and even winter tundra and deserts. Each climate perpetually stays within its productive season, where trees and flowers bloom, and fruit, grain and vegetables thrive. Every animal you know of is present here, as well as many you've never seen. Creatures that have long been extinct roam this place. The Father has made this land as diverse and beautiful as any of His other creations." As Benjamin said this last part, it was obvious that he showed the same kind of pride for Jehovah Yahweh as a child would when telling of some great talent or important position his parent held. It almost seemed like a 'what my dad does for a living' moment for Benjamin.

"It is incredible," Joe agreed, as he caught up to the trio that had been taking the lead for several miles. "I can't get enough of this place. As good as the Sunday School stories were when I was a kid, no words do it justice. As beautiful as the other side was and could be, Heaven is just so much more . . . much more," he trailed off, at a loss for words to describe the intensity and richness of their surroundings. Nothing appeared mundane or boring. Every view was a vista; every moment worth remembering.

As they rode through the countryside, Bud and Slim brought up the rear of the group, engaged in constant conversation. Bud must have known a million jokes and was doing his best to tell all of them. Slim would occasionally add one of his own, providing a sample of his wry, sardonic wit. Hearty laughter rippled through them all like a bubbling stream, punctuated by an occasional groan at an especially corny one-liner. As the brothers took turns entertaining the band of riders, the miles slipped away.

As the group crossed Gad's Way, one of the twelve highways that entered the city, the newly arrived pilgrims that were streaming toward the city gates stared at the mounted group in wonder. It must have looked as if Heaven had been invaded by characters from a Sergio Leone western. As his buckskin clopped across the solid gold bricks of the roadway, Noah raised his hand, as if to tip the brim of an imaginary hat to dark young Indian woman dressed in a vibrant sari. She held the hand of a boy of perhaps five, with the same large black eyes and caramel skin. Kelsie flashed him a brilliant smile and he returned it, showing an impressive set of dimples.

As Gad's Way faded into the distance behind them, the group entered the northern region of Asher. Here, the land began to change; as the savannas they had passed through gave way to landscape that looked remarkably like the American Southwest. Monolithic sandstone mesas rose from the broad plain before them, as thick patches of purple sage, mesquite, and prickly pear in full bloom covered the sandy desert floor. Saguaro cactus raised thick green arms of silent, thorny praise into the deep blue sky, as the riders watched a small group of animals running in the distance, creating a plume of dust that telegraphed their movement.

When the herd of animals drew closer, they appeared to be tiny spotted horses, no bigger than a small dog. Their coats were thick and long, and their feet were tipped by four toes, instead of hooves. They had no mane, and their stubby tails extended from the hind quarters, tipped by a long bush similar to that of a cow's tail. "What in the heck is that?" Noah wondered aloud. "They look like miniature horses, only even more *miniature*."

Kelsie gave him a look of slightly smug confidence, enjoying the idea that she knew the answer to this mystery. "They are called Eohippus, or Dawn Horses. They've been extinct for thousands of years on the other side. I remember them from biology, or the Discovery Channel, or something like that."

"I think I'll stick with Dawn Horses. That 'E-O-Hippo' stuff is a little complicated for my taste," Noah said with a grin.

Kelsie shot him a look. "This coming from a guy that can speak, read and understand any language, play any song on any instrument he picks up, builds houses and motorcycles from scratch, and can throw rainbows from one dimension to another. Somehow I think a Latin name for an ancient species of horse is no big deal."

Noah shrugged. "You can take the boy out of the country…"

"You spent most of your life in the city," Kelsie reminded him.

"The city of *Portland, Tennessee,*" He replied. "It's not exactly Chicago. The highlight of a weekend was to park at the Mapco Mart and compare four wheel drive pickups."

"Point well taken," Kelsie said. "Those were fun times, by the way," she added, with a distant twinkle in her eye.

Noah reached out and took her hand as they rode side by side. "Yes they were, Kelsie. Yes they were."

CHAPTER THIRTY ONE

Verna Lee Booker Hightower stood on a knoll, looking across the frontier, holding her hand to her brow to shade her vision, as her eyes adjusted to shimmering glare if the landscape below. Just within range of her field of vision, a knot of riders had appeared on the horizon. They were coming from the south, and while their progress didn't appear to be rushed, they were making good time. "I think that's the group we've been waiting for from Judah region. I make out six riders. It looks like five men and one woman."

"Six riders?" the little man beside her said, with curiosity in his voice. His accent was a curious mix of East Texas and Parisian French. "There's only supposed to be five. The Emissary must have come with them."

"Makes sense," Verna replied. "They've come from a long way, and I think some of them haven't been here long. They probably haven't been this far north, but the Emissary is taking them on the shortest path, cutting across that gorge to our right. He's obviously familiar with the territory."

The man just nodded. He looked at his traveling companion with admiration, already amazed at skills of observation, even though they had not yet begun to travel together. Verna was a black woman, with long straight hair, a cappuccino complexion and a throaty, alto voice that commanded attention, as well as respect. She had come from a small town in Texas, and had competed as a barrel racer in the Black Rodeo circuit, popular in Texas and Oklahoma during the middle of the twentieth century. She and her husband Ted, had been well known nationally as owners and trainers of some of the finest barrel racing horses in the country. She had raised all six of her children in the saddle, and when she passed over in 1970 at the age of 40, she was known as one of the premiere horsewomen in the country. Standing here now, in gold silk rodeo wear, festooned with diamonds instead of sequins, she looked young, confident and strong. Perhaps that was why she had been selected to lead one of the twelve groups of riders, each group containing twelve riders each.

Verna was also fairly tall, a fact that was not lost on the man that stood beside her, looking up at her regal profile. The man was nearly six inches shorter than this African American cowgirl, but what he lacked in height, he made up for in energy and courage.

The short, thin young man was dressed in a simple white shirt with a Gladstone collar and khaki riding pants, tucked into the tops of his knee high riding boots. His short dark hair was parted in the middle and slicked down, giving him a dapper, if dated look. His name was Nash Turner, and as a fellow Texan, he had been a legend among riders thirty years before Verna was born. But while Verna had earned her spurs in the rodeo, Nash had become famous for what was known as 'the sport of kings' . . . racing thoroughbreds.

Nash had grown up around horses, and given his slight build, as well as his equine affinities, he had made quite a name for himself at the turn of the twentieth century as a celebrity jockey. After gaining notoriety in the United States, he had been invited by an owner to race in France. There, Nash had refreshed his career and his spirit with the change of venue. His subsequent years in Europe had not erased his Texas drawl, but had flavored it with enough French, that he almost sounded like a Louisiana Cajun instead of a transplanted Texan. He had moved on from being a jockey, to a trainer and an owner, until his death in France in 1937. Now, many years later, he retained the curious mixed accent he had acquired on the other side, much as he retained the riding and training skills that made him an ideal candidate for this mission.

As Noah, Kelsie and the rest rode into sight of the gathering group, they could see the pair standing on the knoll, obviously watching for them. The dark skinned girl in a flashy rodeo outfit and the young man that looked no bigger than Benjamin, stood a bit apart from their mounts—a dusty tan quarter horse outfitted with western tack and a black, blaze faced thoroughbred with an English racing saddle. Some distance from them was the larger contingency of riders. Apparently most of them were already here. There seemed to be a hundred or more, dressed in a staggering variety of garb from historical and cultural styles.

As they rode into earshot, Bud shouted a greeting to the pair that were watching from the knoll and threw up his hand. "Come on in! We've been waiting for you!" was the response from the tall, black cowgirl, and gestured for them to proceed. The group kicked the horses into a light gallop and the bounded up the hill to meet the rest of the riders.

Slim was the first make it to the hilltop, and dropped from his saddle easily before the horse came to a complete stop. He grinned at the pair, and introduced himself, as well as the others, as they followed suit and dismounted behind him. "I'm Slim Wilson; this here's my son Joe and my brother, Bud; Bud's grandsons Noah and Benjamin, and Noah's friend Kelsie. We are sorry if we are late. We've come a long ways."

The cowgirl shook her head. "Not at all. We're waiting for a few others that should be along shortly. My name's Verna Lee Booker Hightower; you can just call me Verna. This is Nash Turner," she added, indicating her friend.

"The pleasure is all mine," he said with a flourish and a slight bow as he did so. "Am I to understand you folks are from Tennessee?"

"Middle Tennessee, just north of Nashville, originally," Noah replied. "Most recently from the Judah region. Except for Benjamin here of course," he said, patting his brother on the shoulder. "He lives a little closer to the heart of town, so to speak."

"Of course," Nash said with a knowing chuckle. "Are you going to accompany us on the trip, Benjamin?"

Benjamin blushed a bit. "I'm flattered that you would ask, but no. I just came along for the ride. I will have to be getting back to The Thrones. The Father may have need of me there."

"Oh, that's a pity," Verna said. "I'm sure you would have enjoyed the ride."

"I've already enjoyed the ride," Benjamin replied with a smile. "I'm just glad I don't have to worry about getting saddle sore. This has definitely been a good time," he finished, as he glanced lovingly at his kin.

"When will we see each other again?" Noah asked him. "We've got a few thousand baseballs to catch."

"You'll see me before you know it," Benjamin replied, hugging his brother. "We've got all the time we need."

Benjamin said his goodbyes with hugs all around, and left his horse with Joe, as he turned toward the city. The group watched as he waved a final wave and mounted the Asher Road that led into the gate on the northern side of New Jerusalem. Goodbyes were still a bit wistful to them; but knowing that no goodbye here would ever be permanent in this place dulled the impact of such events.

"Let me fill you in on the expedition," Nash said to them, as they turned to the sound of his voice. "We have twelve groups of twelve riders; each group has a trail boss. Miss Verna here will be the trail boss for our little group, if that's alright with everyone." Noah, Kelsie and the rest nodded their assent as Nash continued. "The other five of our riders are waiting below," he said, indicating five horses grazing placidly and five riders in a rough circle, having a palaver and getting to know each other.

Verna and Nash brought them down the hill and introduced them to what was an extremely diverse group to say the least. There was a Roman soldier in a simple tunic and sandals named Flavius, that had ridden in the Roman army during the first century. He had been converted to Christianity by a prisoner that he had brought to Rome. The man had testified to Flavius of his faith during the journey, and the old soldier had been touched by his sincerity and bravery, even in the face of sure death. As Flavius witnessed the prisoner's violent demise at the hands of a gladiator for the mere entertainment of Roman dignitaries, the peace reflected in the man's eyes had bored into the soldier's soul. He had declared from that moment that he would gladly live such a life and die such a death to serve this prisoner's God. His remaining years on the other side had been spent secretly helping the Christian underground from his position in the military, until he was discovered and executed. Now, he reaped the reward of his faith in Heaven.

Another rider had been an American actor in B-westerns. His name was Alfred "Lash" Larue, and he had been known for his skill with a bullwhip. Bud and Slim were very pleased to meet him, having regarded him as a hero when they were young. The actor had lived an exciting, if somewhat sorted life until he had become a devout Christian during his later years. Noah was pleasantly surprised to discover that Lash had taught Harrison Ford how to handle a whip during his film debut as "Indiana Jones". Lash was humbled and honored that someone would remember his work on the other side, but mostly, glad to be a part of this team, taking on such an exciting task.

The third rider in their group was a taciturn Mongolian nomad by the name of Bazar. Bazar was virtually born in the saddle, riding from the time he was two years old. The only Westerner he had ever met was a missionary that had shared with him the truth of God's love and the promise of this wonderful place. His little brown, shaggy horse seemed no larger than a pony, but it was definitely from hearty stock. Bazar had grown up living on mare's milk and sleeping in felt tents called yurts, roaming the steppes of upper Mongolia. This simple, nomadic lifestyle on the other side made him uniquely suited to the trail drive before him.

Kelsie found a kindred tomboy in the fourth rider, a girl from 14th century Normandy. Her name was Arlette and her parents had died from the bubonic plague when she was eleven. She had survived in the country side, living off the land for a time, concealing her gender, by wearing loose fitting clothing and keeping her chestnut hair cropped short. Arlette, or "Arnesto" as she referred to herself, had managed to pick up work as a stable boy for a local nobleman, sleeping in the barns. As she had grown from a gangly girl into a young woman, the stable groomsman had eventually recognized her deception, and had fallen in love with her. With her secret discovered, she had grown her tresses long and began wearing more feminine clothing, much to the surprise and delight of the groomsman. The two had been wed, and she had spent the rest of her life caring for the master's horses.

The fifth rider was a Spanish conquistador named Pedro Pizarro. Pedro had been a young soldier that came to the New World to serve in name of the crown of Spain and the Church. Upon his arrival, Pedro had been sickened by his superior officer's treatment of the Aztecs, and had vocalized his disdain for the harsh methods used to wipe out the native population. His reward on the other side was the cold steel of an officer's sword, but his reward in Heaven had been much greater. Since his arrival, Pedro had occasionally remarked that if Cortez had seen the gold of Heaven, he would have left the Aztecs alone. "However," he would then finish with a wry smile, "I have not seen Señor Cortez since I have been here. I am thinking he may not have made the journey."

Noah was impressed with all of them, and pleased to see such a variety of cultures represented. He liked Verna, and was happy to take direction from her. She seemed accustomed to leading others, which would only give him and the other riders time to get to know each other. He enjoyed meeting new people and learning new things; this would be a great journey, with plenty of adventurous tales to fill the miles.

The eleven other groups mingled together; some with trail bosses that were famous, many that were virtually unknown. A red headed firebrand named Andrew Jackson led one group. His riders included two Cherokee Indians, a point that Kelsie found ironic, to say the least. Another group was comprised almost entirely of Ottoman Turks that rode majestic Arabian horses. Many cultures had a rich history of horsemanship; those were well represented in the one hundred and forty four member trail drive.

One other American actor arrived shortly after Noah and Kelsie's group. A tall sandy haired fellow strode into the camp, led by a blonde, green eyed girl that was undoubtedly an Emissary. At six foot seven inches tall, he stood a head higher than many of the other riders. He was a newcomer, only recently having come from the other side, and was assigned to a team led by an Australian horse rancher named Harry Suffolk. The tall fellow was accustomed to being thrust into the forefront of service; he had been the first American soldier out of the landing craft at Anzio, Italy on January 22, 1944, since his commanding officer wanted to use his height to gauge the depth of the water. As the newcomer walked past Noah's big buckskin stallion, James Arness patted it on the flank and said to Noah, "Nice horse. I used to ride one just like it."

As the last couple of riders filtered in, the groups lined up in formation, twelve to a group, twelve groups in all. The trail bosses elected Godfrey of Bouillon, a Frankish knight from the Crusades during the first millennium, to take the lead. He rode out in front of the group on a stout, broad built white horse. He turned his mount and addressed the group.

"This group has been chosen by Jehovah Yahweh to undertake the largest drive of horses ever known to man," began Godfrey. "Our King, the only True King, has need of his animals, for a noble purpose only understood by Him alone. While some may speculate, it is not ours to question; it is merely our duty to perform. In Him we live and move and have our being; we were created for His service. Some of you have been selected because of your skill; all of you have been selected because of your heart to serve. We will ride alongside the

Asher Road, leaving it to the pilgrims that enter the city. We will ride into the foothills, where we will follow the New Jordan River into the King's Canyon. There we will find herds of horses belonging to our Mighty Majesty. We will gather them all; every head and hoof, and bring them here. Within the Asher Gate, there are stables that will sufficiently house and care for them."

Godfrey fell silent and gazed about at the formation of mounted riders. A number of newcomers had stopped to watch the spectacle and he nodded toward them graciously. Finally, he raised his head and his voice at the same time, shouting, "Riders! Are you ready?"

With one voice, the one hundred and forty four riders cried, "YES!" The electricity of the moment sent goose bumps through Noah and Kelsie as they flashed a quick grin at each other.

Godfrey nodded in appreciation. "Then let us RIDE!"

CHAPTER THIRTY TWO

The sand beneath the horse's hooves sparkled with the glint of trillions of tiny fragments of jewels. Light filtered through the sparkling dust kicked up by the riders, like an ever changing kaleidoscope of color. The effect cast a rainbow aura around the one hundred and forty four riders as they departed from Asher Road, and began their trek into the high chaparral that led into the King's Canyon.

Ahead in the distance, they could see the New Jordan, winding down from the mountains. Its glittering surface lay embedded in the green hills like a strand of fine silver chain, amid a folded bolt of moss green flannel. Given their reigns, the horse headed toward the water instinctively, giving the riders the opportunity to enjoy the countryside and get to know each other.

Bud, Slim and Lash were finding that they had a lot in common. They apparently shared a flair for showmanship, and talked about the days during which the likes of Roy Rogers and Hop a Long Cassidy inspired boys all over the country to learn to rope, ride and shoot. Nash and Verna rode out front together, deep in conversation, while Joe was forming a surprising bond with Flavius and Bazar. All three shared the same sardonic wit, and enjoyed each other's company on the trail.

Kelsie and Arlette were becoming fast friends, as they rode along together, finding that the archetype of an athletic, strong willed woman had roots in virtually every century of human history. While Arlette explained to Kelsie the particulars of a game from the Middle Ages called handy ball, which sounded as if it were a hybrid of soccer and stickball, Kelsie brought Arlette up to speed on the social and historical condition of the twenty-first century. When the subject turned to relationships, they frequently glanced at Noah and spoke with hushed tones and muted laughs.

While they were out of earshot, Noah tried unsuccessfully to ignore their obvious topic of conversation, his cheeks growing ruddy with each glance. He instead tried to focus on the words of Pedro Pizzaro. Noah found the young soldier to be fascinating, as he told of his travels into the 'New World'. The adventures that Pedro had faced sounded exhilarating for a Tennessee country boy.

"You should have seen the horses when they came off the ship in Mexico," Pedro laughed. "They could not walk. They had developed 'sea legs' during the voyage, and when they hit dry land, they had forgotten how to walk on it. They looked like a drunken sailor," he said, shaking his head and grinning.

"What about the men?" Noah asked. "Could they walk any better?"

"Ah," Pedro replied, "That was different. They actually *were* drunken sailors," he chuckled. "*El Capitan* broke out the rum to celebrate the arrival. They were in worse shape than the horses."

Noah laughed with Pedro, continuing to listen, as the conquistador regaled him with stories. Noah noticed, however, that Pedro never spoke of what happened in Mexico. Finally, he cut to the chase. "Pedro," Noah asked, catching his eye and gazing at him intently, "What was Mexico like?"

Pedro fell silent for a moment, as his mount clopped on. "It was full of beauty," he said finally, "and full of blood."

Noah saw a cloud descent over Pedro's dark, almost black eyes. "If you don't want to talk about it, I understand," he said. "Such things probably shouldn't be mentioned in Heaven."

Pedro gave him a quick look. "On the contrary, *mi hermano,* the depth of the depravity we came from on the other side makes this place all the more *fantastico,*" he replied. "It was just a tragedy on a monumental scale," he continued. "The land was a primitive paradise, and the Aztecs were savage, brutal people in many ways, but they were ignorant, both of God and the riches they possessed. Cortez, de Leon, Garay and the rest claimed to come to this land in the name of 'God' . . . but it was in the name of 'Gold' instead. They slaughtered the native people, and those that didn't die by the musket or the sword, died of diseases brought by our people. It could have been an incredible opportunity to win a nation of people for Christ; instead, our soldiers looted, raped and pillaged in the name of the Church. If there is a travesty worse than all others on the other side, it is this; that men claiming to be children of God abuse those that God wants so desperately to adopt into His true family."

Noah nodded sagely. "My dad told me that Mahatma Gandhi was quoted as saying, 'I would be a Christian, if it were not for Christians.' That's a pretty heavy statement."

"Sadly, so true," Pedro agreed. "But who is this Gandhi fellow?"

"I'm not sure," Noah admitted. "But it sounds like his people were treated like the Aztecs, the Cherokee, the Jews, and a lot of other groups of people over the years."

The expedition continued the ride toward New Jordan River, watching as the river grew larger in their view. The river was about the size of Ohio on the other side, but more shallow, with a mixture of shoals and large areas of rapids, punctuated by occasional smaller deep pools. The metallic brightness faded somewhat as they grew nearer, but the waters still flashed and bubbled with crystal clarity. Large rocks jutted from beneath the surface in many places; the stone outcroppings were primarily a slate gray in color, shot through with thick veins of pink and white quartz. Moss lay in wide swaths on the rocks, while carpets of tiny yellow and lavender wild flowers grew on the banks, watered by the overspray of the rapids.

As they approached the river, Noah rode up alongside Kelsie. "It's beautiful, isn't it? It reminds me of some of the rivers on the other side."

"Yes is does," Kelsie agreed. "It's all different, but it is all so pretty," she breathed.

"Still not as pretty as you," Noah said, gazing at her profile, studying the dusting of freckles across the bridge of her nose, the deep set dimple, and the rounded, high set cheeks. As soon as he said it, he thought how corny it must have sounded. He dropped his head and diluted the moment with a self-deprecating laugh.

Kelsie reached out and lifted his chin until their eyes met. "Hey," she said, smiling as she did so. "Don't try to play that off. That was a good line, and I know what it really meant. For the record, I love you too." She dropped her hand into his and squeezed his fingers. Noah lifted her hand, turned it over and kissed her palm.

"Be careful of such charmers," Nash Turner said to Kelsie as he flanked her on opposite side. "This curly haired one is a bold one, no? In this 'Eden' of a place, a daughter of Eve may want to watch out for a serpent."

"I think we're past that kind of thing," Noah said with a grin. "Thankfully. Besides, there aren't any snakes in Heaven, right?"

Nash nodded. "You are right, my young friend. No snakes. Just like Ireland, Hawaii and New Zealand on the other side. The Heavenly Father has populated this wondrous world with many things, but he left the serpents behind. I suspect He did not want to remind us of the curse of sin that plagued our former lives."

"Fine by me," Verna added, as she neared them and joined the conversation. "I never could stand them; even the ones that weren't poisonous. They may not hurt you, but they would make me hurt myself. Now then, are you both ready to meet the Angel of New Jordan?"

"The who of what?" Noah said quizzically.

"The Angel of New Jordan," Verna repeated. "Each river here has an angel assigned to it, to watch over it and to assist travelers on their way."

"Where is he?" Kelsie asked. "I don't see him."

"You don't see him until you need to," Verna replied. "Godfrey of Bouillon is going to the river to summon him. Come on; let's go see what the angel has to say."

The riders gathered at the river bank and dismounted, allowing the horses to drink their fill of the clear, cold water. They looked into the river, and watched as a school of brown trout swam just beneath the surface of the rapidly running water. One broke the surface with a huge splash and drew applause from a handful of spectators. Someone called for a net and there was a titter of laughter.

As the group quieted, Godfrey and the rest of the trail bosses milled through the riders and gathered at the water's edge. Before them, a monolithic pillar of black translucent onyx stood in the midst of the river. While the stone seemed natural, it was singular in color, shape and size. It was obviously a significant landmark placed there for a purpose.

Godfrey faced the stone and spoke. "We seek the Angel of New Jordan. We are on a quest for Jehovah Yahweh. We seek safe passage and any assistance you may provide. In the name of the Most High, we call upon our fellow servant."

For a moment, nothing happened; everything was quiet, except for the rushing water flowing around the huge slab of inky volcanic glass and the crisp song of a mockingbird in a nearby cottonwood. Then slowly, almost imperceptibly at first, the surface of the black stone seemed to shimmer and ripple, as it took on a fluid quality. A large hand, with skin almost as dark as the stone, parted the surface, thrusting out from the monolith, creating an opening that grew larger as an arm, a shoulder, a head and the rest of a mighty angel followed, stepping from the center of the black onyx column, as easily as one would step out of a shower.

The figure shook rivulets of ebony liquid stone from his face and hair, and as the drops left him, they solidified again instantly, scattering as a circle of smooth black pebbles in the river around him. The angel was black skinned and tall, standing upon the surface of the water as if it were frozen solid beneath his bare feet. His features were Nubian, with a broad, flat nose, a heavy brow, and tightly kinked hair that was trimmed to a well kept afro of about two inches in uniform length. His gaze was intense and unyielding, and when he spoke, his voice sounded like a chorus of baritones talking in perfect unison.

"I am the Angel of New Jordan," he said. "My name does not matter to you; I serve the One Great God, the Mighty Everlasting Father, Jehovah Yahweh."

Godfrey bowed and bent a knee as if to kneel; many others of the riders prepared to follow his example. The angel's right arm shot out suddenly and he raised his massive hand. "Stop!" he shouted. "Do not bow to me, or kneel before me, for I am not worthy. I am your fellow servant and will assist you as well as I am able. What is it you seek?"

Godfrey caught himself, rose and regained his composure. "We have been sent to retrieve Jehovah Yahweh's horses. We seek the King's Canyon. Can you help us?"

The angel nodded slowly. "Yes, I can. I must remain at my post here, but I will tell you the way. This great river flows from the mountains above. It has many branches and tributaries. You will follow the main channel, until you reach a triune fork. From there, you will cross New Jordan and take the branch that is furthest right. That is Trinity River. You will then follow it upstream through a narrow valley, where an adjoining stream appears to flow from a sheer cliff of red stone. That cliff is the Crimson Veil; you will ride directly through the Veil; there you find the King's Canyon. I wish you peace, Godspeed and a successful journey."

With that, the angel turned, walked back to the monolith, and walked into the stone column, as easily as he had stepped from it. The stone enveloped his form, and solidified once again, not leaving the slightest trace of the angel's exit or return.

"Well, *that* was interesting," Noah remarked to no one in particular. "How are we supposed to cross the river? How are we supposed to ride 'through' a stone cliff?"

Nash Turner stepped between Noah and Kelsie and placed a hand on Noah's shoulder. "If there is one thing I have learned since I have been here *mon frere*, is that even in Heaven, everything is not always as it appears to be."

CHAPTER THIRTY THREE

T he New Jordan took the group of riders on a meandering path into the foothills of the mighty range of mountains that encircled the land of Heaven. The landscape had become lush and green again as they gained altitude and left a wide swath of somewhat dry chaparral behind. Wildlife was abundant, and as they watched a puma padding along a ledge above them at one point, Kelsie was reminded of the two panthers that had traveled with them when they first arrived in the land. It seemed like a lifetime ago, and yet she realized, they had only just begun the eternal adventure of Heaven. How amazing, how grand the scope of things! It still challenged her heart and imagination, and she thought it probably always would.

As they climbed, Noah wondered to himself if Heaven was situated on a globe, like a planet, and after a discussion with Kelsie on the subject, they both agreed that it probably wasn't. Since Heaven was a spiritual place, beyond the constructs and experiences of mankind, they decided that it did not have to follow the physical laws and scientific reason of the other side. They had already experienced how easily this spiritual life contradicted the ideas of gravity, mass, volume, entropy and kinetic energy. They knew that although they ate and drank from the land for the sheer pleasure of it, they really were never hungry or weak; they really needed no physical nourishment.

The power of this land seemed to be limited only by the imagination of those living in it. Even the animals that God had populated into this land, needed no care, no feeding. The horses might graze the thick grass or drink from the cold clear water of the river, but it was apparent that they had no more need of these physical things than the men and women did. *As we grow accustomed to Heaven in the millennia to come,* Noah thought, *I wonder how far the stretched boundaries of our imagination will take us.*

As if in response to his thoughts, Noah felt a vibration, a thrumming within the scabbard of the sword worn at his side. He halted for a moment, letting others riders pass, as he drew the blade from its sheath. Sure enough, the hilt pulsed in his hand, and as he rested the tip on his other palm, he felt the warm, living sensation of the transparent metal's movement. As he peered into the layers of steel and the thousands of words engraved there, one phrase fairly leapt from it metal depths, searing into his mind:

"Thou shalt see greater things than these." (John 1:50, KJV)

Greater things . . . greater things . . . the words of Jesus. What greater things? How much greater? Noah was entranced by the thought.

255

"You okay?" Bud asked, as he turned his mount and looked back at Noah. "You look like you're a million miles away."

More like a million years away, Noah thought, as he discreetly slid his sword back into its scabbard. "Just getting a little inspiration," he replied with a crooked grin, and coaxed the tall buckskin into a trot to catch Bud, Kelsie and the others.

The riders rode into a gorge that opened into a wide valley in the high country. As the valley spread out before them, they could see that the New Jordan was fed by two smaller rivers that entered from either side. The river closest to them was the Azure, so named because of the river bed covered in pale, sky blue stone. It looked as if the northern sky was melting at some higher elevation beyond their vantage point and pouring into the banks that flowed around to their left, blocking their path.

Straight ahead, lay the New Jordan, its broad channel bisecting the valley more or less equally. Interestingly, as they looked up stream, the New Jordan seemed quieter, more placid. Its waters lay still, with a glass like surface that barely rippled with the gentle flow of millions of gallons of water.

To the furthest right, raging out of the northeast, was the Azure's and New Jordan's smaller, wilder sister, the Trinity. The Trinity River was half the size of the Azure, but one look let the riders know what waters gave the lower rapids of the New Jordan their life. The Trinity burst forth in a torrent, from a deep, narrow channel cut in vivid red sandstone. The current was swift enough to roll stones along beneath the surface; they were large enough to be seen from the rider's vantage point downstream, on the bank below the Azure.

"The Triune Fork," Pedro Pizzaro breathed, obviously impressed by its beauty and complexity. "It would be a wonderful adventure to follow the path each of these to their source."

"Unfortunately, we don't have that luxury, Pedro," Verna Lee said with a friendly, but firm smile. "There will always be time. Right now, we have to follow that wild little rapid and see where it goes. I doubt that many have come this way before."

"I don't know that any have come this way before," Slim replied, as he reigned up with Noah, Kelsie and the rest of Verna's group. "We haven't come across any newcomers traveling out of the mountains since we entered this valley."

Kelsie looked around in sudden realization. "That's true. I haven't seen anyone but the riders for twenty miles or more."

Nash Turner smirked a bit as he paraphrased Frost, "Three rivers diverged in a valley and I, I took the one less traveled by, and that has made all the difference."

"What I'm interested in more than knowing who's been here before, is knowing how and where we intend to cross," Verna said. "I better go talk to the trail bosses and see what they intend to do." With that, she rode out to a clearing on the bank, where the other trail bosses had gathered.

After some animated deliberation, Godfrey stepped out from the group of leaders and addressed the rest of the riders. "Since there is no bridge, we have decided that we should swim the horses across here, where the river has become one channel. It is deeper and broader of course, but the horses are strong, and as we know, there appears to be no danger for this course of action."

Noah looked at the rest and they seemed resigned to follow that course of action. But for him, something just didn't feel right, so he raised his hand to get Godfrey's attention. "Yes?" Godfrey recognized his signal. "Do you have something?"

"Well yeah, actually I do," Noah replied, as the others turned to listen. A tinge of color crept into his cheeks as they did so. "I apologize if this seems stupid, but instead of swimming the horses across, why don't we just walk them across?"

Godfrey and several others looked confused. "That would be fine, young man, if we had a bridge. But there seems to be no place to walk them."

Noah smiled at this, and thought to himself that he was about to either look like a genius or a fool. "Begging your pardon, but we are King's children on a ride through the King's land to the King's Canyon. I don't believe we need a bridge." With that, Noah leaned forward, whispered into his horse's ear and urged him toward the river's edge. When the horse's hooves reached the water, he hesitated for a moment, until Noah urged him forward again. Then, the buckskin stepped out on the surface of the water, and the water held the horse and rider's weight as easily as water skipper glides upon the surface tension of a small stream.

The horse took a few cautious tentative steps, before Noah reined it around to face the rest of the riders. "As you can see," he said beaming, "We have the opportunity to step out on faith."

"Bravo," Godfrey said with a laugh, clapping slowly as he did so. "You have followed the example of Peter, with substantially better results, my friend. Your name is Noah, is it not?"

Noah nodded in affirmation. "Well riders," Godfrey said with a smile, "Let us follow Noah's example and *walk* our horses across the river."

The riders crossed, on either side of Noah, as his horse stood upon the surface of the river. Joe muttered a wisecrack about feeling like Wiley Coyote running off a cliff, and Kelsie playfully called Noah a showoff under her breath as she passed near him, but it was a significant moment in the journey. Trail bosses and riders alike looked at Noah in a new light. Through conversations on the trail, many of them had learned of he and Kelsie's passing on the other side and had known how young they were. Now, they saw Noah as more than a teenager; he was a man, with a man's skill, leadership and faith.

This collective attitude was no more evident than when they had all crossed the river and reconvened upstream at the mouth of the Trinity River. Godfrey and the rest of the trail bosses dismounted and spoke briefly among themselves, occasionally gesturing toward Noah. Finally, as a consensus was reached, Godfrey strode across to Noah and Kelsie. "You have shown us a talent and courage for leadership today, Noah. We have decided that we would like you to lead this expedition the rest of the way, if you are willing."

Noah was thunderstruck. These men and women were leaders; heavy hitters from throughout history and the world. There was a former general and American president in the group; the man standing before him had led armies during the Great Crusades. "I don't know what to say, sir," he began. "I'm honored that you would ask. But there are more experienced leaders here, with reputations for success and victory."

"But none of us displayed the faith that you did today," Godfrey replied. "And here, faith is the key. We must have confidence in our

Creator and the incredible work He has done in us, and we are all still learning that, even here. But you, Noah, you showed us a taste of those capabilities. Will you lead us? Will you take us to the King's Canyon and bring those horses back to New Jerusalem?" He extended a hand to Noah.

Noah looked at Kelsie, as she nodded to him, encouraging him to step up. He looked into the eyes of the Crusader before him and felt a new passion, a new authority, a new responsibility grow in his heart. *Greater things . . . .*

Noah took Godfrey's hand and shook it. "With God's help, I will lead." With that, Noah turned on his heel, thrust his right boot into the stirrup, grabbed the horn of the saddle, and swung his left leg across his mount. He gazed at one hundred and forty three faces that looked upon him with expectation and anticipation. With a flourish and a metallic singing ring, he drew his sword and held it high above his head as he cried with a new confidence in his voice, "FOR THE KING! TO THE CRIMSON VEIL! LET US RIDE!"

CHAPTER THIRTY FOUR

The wind whistled up the narrow slot canyon as Noah led the group of riders alongside the roaring torrent of the twisted little Trinity River. The water created a cool mist that rose from its froth; the cold, almost refrigerated temperature of the river indicated that its source was probably either subterranean or coming from snowmelt on the mountains above. The surroundings were dotted with thick groves of Blue Spruce and Ponderosa Pine. If the group had not known better, the landscape looked much like the western slope of the Rockies in Colorado.

Noah rode with the trail bosses, as did Kelsie. They all seemed very accepting of Noah's leadership role, as well as Kelsie's presence. Their close relationship was obvious; no one questioned the idea that she would ride with him. As they rode, she got to know Verna and listened as the African American barrel racer spoke of her husband, her children and her life in Texas on the other side. Kelsie talked about her family, her school, and her life growing up in the hills and hollows of Tennessee.

A tall, rail thin Tennessean rode by Noah for several miles, his ramrod straight posture revealing his military bearing. The rider's thick shock of unruly hair was almost the same shade of red as Kelsie's, and his countenance was determined, as if he meant business.

"Tell me, Noah," the ginger haired rider began. "I hear you are from the Nashville area, and that you lived there during the twenty first century. What can you tell me of Tennessee in your time?"

Noah eyed him carefully, and answered his question with another question. "You're Jackson aren't you? I recognize you from the history books. The portraits I've seen were from when you were older, but I know the face."

The man smiled and nodded. "I'm afraid those pictures were either painted in a good light by those that would have curried favor with me, or by my enemies to put as many flaws on the canvas as possible. After several battles and a lifetime of public service, I am happy that God has saw fit to wash away the worry lines on my face along with the sin in my soul."

"I cannot begin to imagine what your life must have been like," Noah replied.

"Nor yours," Jackson said. "You have seen things that people of our time only dreamed of."

"True," Noah said thoughtfully, "Tennessee in my time has over six million people. The largest cities are Nashville, Knoxville, Memphis and Chattanooga. There are paved highways everywhere and horseless carriages called automobiles all over the place. You can travel from Nashville to Knoxville by road in three hours; to Memphis in three and a half. There are airports, where machines called airplanes can fly like birds, only at hundreds of miles an hour. There are devices called cell phones that pretty much everyone carries, that enable you to carry on a conversation anywhere in the world. Music, pictures and plays that we call movies can be recorded on machines no bigger than your thumb and replayed anytime. Nashville is a cultural capital with art, music and sports, and they have some of the best hospitals in the country. Medical care has gotten so good that they can take out a person's heart, repair it, and put it back in. Our country has sent people into space; men have walked on the moon. It is hard to imagine how different it is from your time."

Jackson's eyes twinkled with wonder. "Amazing, truly amazing. It sounds almost as incredible as this place."

Noah snorted derisively. "Hardly. Sin still abounds. People are still the same. There are probably less true Christians in our time than in yours. Folks are never happy, no matter what they have. Men and women in the twenty first century live longer and have more than ever before, but it is still a miserable, cursed existence. There have been two world wars and a slew of others; drug, alcohol and sex addiction are rampant, people abuse children, starve each other, kill for nothing. Government is a scandalous mess. Society is openly blasphemous and ignores God in anything and everything. The end is near; it has to be."

Jackson nodded grimly. "I wonder if it will be the end for the United States, or for everything. It sounds as if the situation is probably as grave in other parts of the world."

"It is global," Noah said. "The whole thing is messed up. And with the world wide communication available in my time, everyone is able to talk to everyone. That may sound like a good thing, but the last time the world spoke with one voice, it was at the Tower of Babel; and you know what happened there."

"God confounded the language of the people because they had become so 'enlightened,' they believed they could act without Him," Jackson replied. "If I recollect, I believe God said, 'Behold, the people is one, **And now nothing will be restrained from them that they have imagined to do.'**(Genesis 11:6, KJV) That's a frightening thought."

Noah agreed. "Just because you have the liberty and the ability to do something, doesn't mean you should."

Jackson smiled. "I think you could have been a president."

Noah smirked. "A politician? No thanks. I'd rather be a country boy from Tennessee."

Phillip D. Wilson

"Me too, Noah," Jackson said, smiling. "Me too."

As the riders carefully walked their horses up a steep, grassy slope that took them sharply around a rock ledge to the left, they were surprised to see the slope drop off the other side, giving way to a wide, shallow lake that lay in a basin, beneath a huge, sheer cliff of deep red sandstone. The water flowed from its base, seemly bubbling from beneath the rock, filling the basin, until it spilled over the rim, beginning its lively descent into the valleys the riders had just come through.

"The Crimson Veil," Kelsie said, as she stopped beside Noah, still mounted on her horse. "Very cool . . . and very, uh, sheer."

The cliff rose several hundred feet before them, with vertical striations in the color that made the face look like a pleated curtain of stone. It glistened with moisture from the mist that rose from the face of the lake. A reflection of the cliff shimmered on the face of the water, making it appear to extend all the way to the rim of the basin.

Godfrey rode up with a few others and dismounted, as Noah and Kelsie stepped out of the saddle as well. "Well, my friend," Godfrey inquired, "Have you given any thought to where we go from here? I am confident in your ability to lead us, most assuredly; I am just interested in the where and the how."

"As am I," Noah said. "This cliff is massive. Is the King's Canyon above it, below it, or around it?"

"The angel said we were to go *through* it," Kelsie replied. "I believe we can; I've seen us do some amazing things with the stone, wood and other materials around us with just our will. But how far will we have to go? This stone looks miles thick. Are we going to have to plow a mountain pass through it?"

Noah shook his head, studying the rock face. "I don't think so. Something is off about this; I just can't put my finger on it."

Noah thought about what Nash Turner had said earlier. *Even in Heaven, everything is not always what it appears to be.* The Crimson Veil appeared massive and vertical. Its face was sheer, without as much as a handhold. Wait a second. *Sheer . . .* that has more than one meaning, Noah thought. It means straight, clean, complete, but it also means thin . . . transparent. *Like a veil.*

Noah thought about the stories he had heard in church about the veil that hung between the outer court of the temple and the Holy of Holies. He thought about how it was supposed to be woven from linen, strong and impenetrable, but on the day that Jesus was crucified, it was ripped in two, from top to bottom, representing open access to God through the sacrifice of Christ. *The veil is open,* a voice inside his heart said. *It always has been for those that will enter.* "Come on," he said to Kelsie. "Let's go check this out."

They both mounted their horses, while the remainder of the riders waited and watched. As before, Noah nudged his buckskin forward with a gentle tap of his boot heels. The horses stepped onto the glassy surface of the lake, and as before, their hooves stood easily and firmly upon the water. Not even a ripple was present.

They rode gently, slowly and deliberately toward the face of the cliff. As they neared the Crimson Veil, the stone seemed to shimmer, like an image seen through a heat wave on a hot day. Noah's buckskin plodded along, as if there was no obstruction before him whatsoever; Kelsie's horse followed close behind. Then, as Noah's horse reached the cliff, it reached out with its nose as if to touch the red rock wall and horse's head abruptly disappeared.

The effect was so startling, that Noah hauled back on the reins. As he did so, the horse turned and his head emerged once again from the cliff. As it stepped sideways, alongside the rock face, Noah reached out his hand tentatively. It also disappeared into what felt like a cold, wet mist. *It's an illusion,* Noah thought. *It's not really there.*

He looked at Kelsie and grinned. "It's like a rainbow, reflected on the mist of the lake, only it just mirrors the rock face on either side of the canyon. We can ride right through it." He called to the others. "Come on! It's just an optical illusion! We can ride right through!" With that, Noah pulled the nose of his horse back around and rode through the Veil.

As he and Kelsie entered the Veil, they saw the red cliff walls that stood on either side of them, creating the effect that they had seen on the other side of the Veil. The walls opened up quickly however, as before them lay a canyon carved by God, watered by several small springs that ran together and became the Trinity River. The canyon was terraced in layers of meandering topography, stretching for miles outward and upward, framed by the rim of mountain peaks above. The landscape was dappled with color from a thousand shades of greens, tans, reds, and a dazzling display of wildflowers. Thickets of raspberries, cobbler berries and bush beef gave way to groves of aspen, birch, ash and lodge pole pine. Their magnitude was breathtaking; The King's Canyon was truly one of the great wonders of Heaven.

On a broad shelf of grass covered stone five hundred feet above them in elevation, a herd of several hundred magnificently brilliant white horses stood and watched them. Their coats were shiny and slick, as if they had been brushed; their manes and tails were long, thick and wavy. As Noah and Kelsie sat atop their mounts admiring the beauty, the other riders filtered through the Veil with awestruck expressions.

Kelsie looked around and caught the eye of her friend Arlette and the two exchanged glances as if to say, 'I know, right? It's amazing'.

Noah's eyes fixed on a stallion that stood at the head of the herd. He was larger that many of the others, and appeared to be the alpha male of the group. As their eyes met, the big stud looked at Noah as if he knew what he and the riders were there for. "Well, here we are, big boy," Noah said to himself, as he looked into those intelligent, fierce eyes. "And we're coming to bring you back home. You and your friends have a job to do."

CHAPTER THIRTY FIVE

O ne hundred and forty four riders lined up in twelve columns of twelve beside the Trinity River, just inside the mouth of the King's Canyon. They looked upward and ahead at the expansive landscape around them; its beauty and scope gave it the appearance of a country all unto itself. If someone had told them the rest of Heaven had been a dream and that this place alone was really the storied Promised Land, it would have been easy to believe. The vistas were breathtaking; the size larger than any of them would have guessed.

Jackson and Godfrey rode out to speak with Noah. "Well, my friend, how do you propose that we cover this unmitigated wilderness?" Godfrey asked. "As gorgeous as it is, it is also vast. It is quite a job for such a small troop of riders."

Jackson agreed. "Yes, I would venture to say that if we spread out singly, we could spend the equivalent of a year or more and never see another rider. With the overwhelming odds of such a task, I find myself wishing we could consult Gideon for his input about succeeding with the three hundred men God gave him."

Noah smiled faintly. "Ironically, I guess we could have done just that, if we had thought of it. But we're here now, and we have to take on the job at hand, with the people we have. Father God must have called all that we need, so it can't be as hard as it seems."

A voice from behind them interjected an agreement into the conversation. "If we can ride on water, seems to me that we can do whatever we need," Bud Wilson said, as he and Kelsie walked up on either side of Noah. "Chief, you've done pretty well by following your heart and acting in faith. What does your heart tell you about this?"

Noah's eyes searched the distant hills, where he had seen a herd of white horses earlier. They had moved from his sight, but the trails he saw lacing the vegetation indicated that the hills were well inhabited by the animals and that catching sight of them would not be difficult. "I believe these horses are subject to their owner. I think that this depends on another act of will. If we find them and lead them, they will follow."

"And how to you suppose we lead them?" Jackson queried.

"In another life," Bud said, "I would have just called them. We used to stand on the side of a hill and holler up the creek for the cattle. If you could get a good echo going, every cow on the place would come trotting down to the barn.

"Have you ever called a horse?" Kelsie asked, with a tinge of trepidation in her voice.

"Well, no," Bud admitted, "But we had a few horses and most of the time, the horses would come along with the cows; they were a little more skittish, but they traveled with the same herd mentality."

"Actually, I've seen the Creek Indians do it," Jackson replied. "They had calls for them; but I think it would depend on training and familiarity. They would have to at least know the voice."

Kelsie looked at Noah. "If God's sheep know His voice, maybe His horses do too; if not His voice, maybe His music." Her comment caused an instant sparked of recognition between them; Noah nodded with excitement.

"Kelsie's onto something," Noah replied. "Maybe music, like songs of praise and worship would draw them in."

Bud shrugged. "It's worth a try. Why don't you, pull that fancy little guitar off your saddle pack and give it a shot."

Noah agreed and unfastened the leather straps that held his guitar on top of the rear of his saddle. He worked a Fender medium guitar pick out of his jean's pocket with his thumb, and strummed a tentative "G" chord. He twisted the tuning pegs, dialing in a couple of wayward strings, and tried again; this time it rewarded him with a perfect, resonant sound. "What sounds good-classical, country, contemporary?"

Godfrey thought about it for a moment and made a proposal. "How about something that might be 'traditional' to Heaven. You wouldn't know anything in Hebrew, by chance?"

Noah flashed him a quick, confident smile. "Well I could do anything in Hebrew, just like any of the rest of us. We all speak it as easily as any other language. But I did pick up a traditional Hebrew folk song from a friend at the Music Guild; let's see what that does." Taking a moment to recall the tune, Noah hit a chord and began singing in perfect Hebrew:

Hallelujah la-'olam
Hallelujah yashiru kulam
Be-mila 'akhat bodeda
Ha-lev male be-hamon toda
Ve-holem gam hu: 'eyze 'olam nifla

Hallelujah 'al hakol
Halelu 'al makhar ve-'etmol
Hallelujah u-tnu yad be-yad
Ve-shiru bi-lev ekhad – Hallelujah!

Hallelujah 'im ha-shir
Hallelujah 'al yom she-me'ir
Hallelujah 'al ma she-haya
U-ma she-'od lo haya – Hallelujah!

When he took a break, Kelsie picked up the tune, translating the words into English:

Hallelujah, sing a song
Hallelujah, we'll follow along
With a simple word, a single word
We'll bless the sky, the tree, the bird
And we'll fill our heart with joy
Hallelujah!

Hallelujah, hand in hand
Hallelujah, all over the land
Hallelujah, let's try from the start
And sing it with all our heart
Hallelujah!

Hallelujah, sounds of love
Hallelujah, the sunshine above
Hallelujah, the bells will go ringing
And echo from dawn 'till night
Hallelujah!

As Kelsie finished her last 'Hallelujah', Godfrey pointed ahead of them and in a forced whisper, *"Look- it's working!"*

The group looked at the rock shelf that laid at a slightly diagonal elevation two hundred feet above them. A majestic white stallion, followed by forty or fifty more horses stood listening to the music. As Godfrey and Jackson indicated for Noah and Kelsie to continue, Noah began playing again and the two sang the song through once more. As they sang, the horses slowly descended and closed the gap between them and the riders. As the small herd drew near, the riders could see a brand across each horse's right rear flank. The brand was Greek "alpha" symbol, followed by the "omega" symbol, with a diagonal crucifix bisecting the other two characters. The brands looked fresh and clean, with crisp, defined lines.

The horses themselves were beautiful, and while each animal was distinctive, they all shared common traits. Their coats were glossy and as white as any horse the riders had ever seen. The manes and tails looked as if they had been brushed and trimmed, flowing in long wavy locks. Finally, each horse had pale blue eyes, a characteristic commonly known as 'glass eyes'. It was a rare variation, and seeing a herd of horses that all stared at them with those pale eyes together was vaguely unsettling. They seemed intelligent, almost sentient. But the one that stood in front was obviously the alpha male of the herd.

"Hello my friend," Noah said quietly, as he looked into the big stallion's eyes and walked slowly toward him. "I have come a long way to meet you. I'm not here to hurt you; I'm here to ask you and your friends to come with me. You have a job to do, and your Creator has need of you." He stretched out his hand, and offered a dvash fruit in his open palm. The big animal sniffed it, studied Noah for a moment, and plucked the fruit from his hand. As the stallion crunched the fruit, Noah ran a hand across his withers, and the horse's coat twitched briefly. A throaty neigh came from deep in the beast's chest.

"Looks like you've got a friend," Kelsie said. "You got a name for him?"

Noah shook his head. "I've got a feeling if he has a name, it's not mine to give. When his master speaks his name, he will know." He ran his fingers through the majestic animal's mane and smiled before turning to the Jackson, Godfrey and the rest of the trail bosses. "We need to get the rest of these horses together. How many singers and musicians do we have?"

"I'm sure I've heard most of our riders humming some tune or another during the trip," Godfrey replied. "We have quite a number of musicians carrying guitars, harps and mandolins. I even saw one playing a . . . what did he call it? Oh yes, a harmonica."

Bud Wilson grinned. "That would have been me," he said, produced a small silver instrument from his shirt pocket. "I played when I was a kid and picked it up again when I got here."

"Apparently," Jackson said, "the Heavenly Father has once again provided us with something we didn't even know we would need. We assumed that these men and women were selected because of their skills in the saddle. It never occurred to me that we might have such a strong contingent of singers and band members. Now what do you propose we do with them?"

It was evident that Noah had a plan. "Each group of twelve will stay together and take a bearing from the left most canyon wall to the right most canyon wall. The groups will be spread out across the land and will ride as deep as they think they need to; that will have to be the trail boss's call. The groups will sing and play every song of praise and worship, every hymn and every tune that they can think of that lifts up the Lord. Take turns; this will take a while. If you run out of something to sing, make it up as you go. If I'm right, the horses should come out of the hills and follow you without even having to herd them. When you think you've gone as deep into the canyon as you need to, bring them back to the Crimson Veil. We'll wait until everyone is here, and we will head back to New Jerusalem."

"How will we know that we've got them all?" Verna Lee Booker Hightower asked.

Noah just gave her a quick wink and smiled. "The same way we've made it this far. You just gotta have faith."

Chapter Thirty Six

Dekel had been on post as a guard by the Asher Road since his last assignment on the other side. During that period in time, he had seen the depravity that humans could sink to, when they succumbed to the temptation of sin and selfishness. He had seen brother rise against brother during the bloody years of the American Civil War, fighting over the barbaric practice of selling human beings. He had held a child as her mother, wasted by starvation and disease, had been marched into the gas chambers at Auschwitz, in an effort to wipe the children of Abraham off the face of the earth. He had stood over a dying soldier that was no more than a boy, as he made his final peace with God on the beach at Normandy, less than three minutes after the same soldier had stepped onto the sand and into a hail of gunfire.

When the soldier stepped into Heaven, Dekel walked with him and never returned to the other side. He had served on the other side for seven hundred years and when he asked for another assignment, and he was given this post. While some angels might crave action, he found that he liked this work quite well. The location was, well, it was Heaven. A post doesn't get much better than that. He found that he enjoyed being a guide for those that needed direction. He liked meeting the sons and daughters of man as they made their journey into the city, eyes filled with wonder, still overwhelmed by the splendor of their surroundings. It was only when the crowds thinned somewhat, that he found his mind wandering. Even angels daydream, and during this time, as there had been a lull in the pilgrims passing through, Dekel found his thoughts drifting.

"Are you asleep over there?" The angel across the highway boomed. "Or are you counting bricks in the highway?" A taunting smile graced his otherwise fierce looking face. "I don't want you falling out and crushing an unsuspecting pilgrim." Sefer had held his post nearly as long as Dekel, and the two enjoyed a bit of friendly banter, as well as conversation of the more serious variety, when traffic on the highway was slow.

Dekel chuckled. "Haven't you ever heard of sleeping like an angel?" he quipped.

"Such a remark usually refers to a sweet little human infant, and I don't think you're exactly little . . . or sweet for that matter," Sefer said sardonically.

"Hey, that hurts," Dekel said, feigning an offended expression. "I'm as sweet as honey."

"Well you may draw a few flies, anyway," Sefer shot back.

Dekel and Sefer had both picked up a sarcastic sense of humor from the extensive time they had spent with the sons and daughters of men.

Many of their angel brethren strove to avoid picking up the cultural characteristics of humans, but it was hard to avoid when you spent so much time with them. Moreover, they knew that most angels secretly admired humans, in spite of their frailties and shortcomings. Yes, they all fell short of the glory of God; they were all fashioned from the same sin cursed earth. They could be weak, twisted, cruel, selfish and thoughtless. They could be monsters, enslaving others, molesting children, killing for no apparent rhyme or reason.

But for every monster, there were a hundred or more heroes; men and women that pressed toward the mark of the high calling God had placed upon them. There were extraordinary figures that made their mark in the annals of history. But there were also so many more that the world would never know. Ordinary people that lived extraordinary lives; they gave, acted and lived obediently and sacrificially. No one would ever erect a bronze statue to the harried housewife that struggled to make ends meet and keep the tenuous bond of her family together while her husband wallowed in the throes of profound alcoholism. No medals would be given to the sharecropper that managed to scrape together enough meager wages to feed and clothe his family in the midst of the Great Depression. These common folk were forgotten by human history; but to the angels that had witnessed their fiber and determination, these ordinary people were valiant, strong and as tough as flint.

As the two guardian angels enjoyed needling each other on their post, a thought began to tug at Dekel's attention; a wheedling little idea that something was a bit off, but it was something that he couldn't put his finger on. "Sefer," he finally asked, "Have you noticed anything odd?"

Sefer shrugged. "Not really," was his reply.

Dekel stepped from the highway's edge to its center and turned to peer up the thoroughfare toward the mountains. "We haven't seen any pilgrims in quite some time. The traffic gets a bit thin every once in a while, but the road is empty."

Sefer walked across and stood beside his fellow guard. "Now that you mention it, you're correct. I wonder what could have stopped the flow. You know people have to still be coming over. Jehovah Yahweh has decreed that it is appointed to man once to die, then the judgment; and that's an appointment they all have to keep."

"I don't think they've stopped coming," Dekel said, gazing past Sefer's shoulder and pointing into the distance. "They are just staying off the road. You see that group there? They are headed for the city, but something's made them take a detour." Sure enough, Sefer turned to see a sizable party of pilgrims in the distance, wandering across the landscape of the Asher region, cutting across to the city beyond.

As the two puzzled angels stood in the middle of the deserted paved highway, they began to feel a distant vibration beneath their feet. The vibration was steady and rhythmic, becoming stronger, until it became a rumble that could be heard as well as felt. They turned in the direction of the mountains, where the sound seemed to originate, and far down the highway, they saw a glimmer of movement. It first looked like a silver heat shimmer that stretched across the width of the highway like a broad curtain, but as it drew nearer, the vision made it clear what the rumble was; it was the sound of millions of hoofbeats.

A gleaming white multitude of horses thundered down the highway as far as the eye could see, coming from the foothills of the majestic snowcapped mountains. The massive herd looked like an avalanche, a runaway wall of snow and ice, consuming the golden highway with an insatiable appetite. Dotted along the front edge was a row of mounted riders, leading the way.

"They're the sons and daughters of man we saw headed out on the mission," Dekel declared. "They are bringing Jehovah Yahweh's horses from the King's Canyon."

The angel's eyes met for a moment, considering the implications. "Sound the shofar, my brother," Sefer said with a smile. "We must let the other guardians know. Things are about to get interesting."

The two angels resumed their post and Dekel pulled a curled ram's horn from his belt called a shofar, and pressed the mouthpiece to his lips. As he blew the trumpet, the sound echoed for miles down the Asher Road, all the way to the gates of New Jerusalem. Every angel drew his sword and held it aloft in salute, as the mighty herd of horses approached. As the blades were drawn from their scabbards, they glowed with tongues of intense blue flame. The effect was one of a supernatural landing strip, with all the lights on, ready for the landing of an important cargo.

The trail bosses rode twelve abreast in front, with Noah and Kelsie leading, front and center. The rest of the riders were spaced out along the sides, with two groups bringing up the rear. As they looked down the road at the guardian angels holding their flaming swords aloft, they were thunderstruck by the welcome. "Looks like a big deal," Kelsie said, shooting a sidelong glance at Noah. "Think that committee's for us?"

"Either us, or them," Noah replied, nodding over his shoulder at the herd of horses bearing down on them. "No matter what, they better open the barn door . . . the King's horses are coming home."

CHAPTER THIRTY SEVEN

The King's Stables covered over four thousand acres on both sides of the highway, just inside the Asher Gate in New Jerusalem. Constructed of ash and black granite, with trim apportioned in gold filigree and embellishments of various precious jewels, the grounds of the stable were finer than any home on the other side. The fact that they were built to house animals rather than people helped to drive home the splendor and glory of the city. The facilities were laid out in neat rows of thousands of pens and stables, with exercise yards spaced periodically throughout the grounds.

Several thousand people had been recruited to staff and prepare the facilities, each one of them having been a rider, a trainer or other member of the equine community in their past life. They had lovingly covered the floors with fresh cedar shavings and clean straw; they stocked the feed stores with heaps of fragrant alfalfa and fat sacks of oats. Hundreds of tack rooms dotted the layout, stocked with new bridles, saddles, blankets, and various equestrian paraphernalia. The facility was fully prepared and completely new; no horse had ever been stabled there, and the workers that had prepared it were excited at the news that the King's horses would make this their new home.

As the massive herds of beautiful white horses poured through the gates, the stable workers opened gates and directed the flow on a grand scale. The movement of this much livestock was greater than any operation in human history. No railhead, feedlot or stockyard had ever received this many horses in a decade, much less at one time. Still, the horses clopped along, trotting into place as if they had been created for this place, this purpose and this time. Most of the trail drive riders sat mounted on the sidelines and watched the operation with a sense of wonder and satisfaction.

Noah, Kelsie, Bud, Slim and Joe, sat perched on a fence rail, drinking in the success of the operation. "Well praise God," Slim said with a crooked smile. "I'm honored and humbled that He allowed me to be a part of such a grand scheme. All my life, I've never been anything but an old cattle trader and cowboy at heart, and as good as Heaven has been to me these past few decades, this is one of the most fulfilling things I've ever done."

"I hear ya," Bud agreed. "And getting to do this with my brother, my nephew, my grandson and..." he paused a moment, giving Kelsie a grin, "My new granddaughter has been the best part. I've seen more territory during this trip than I ever did in my entire life, but knowing that it was for God's glory and getting to do the job with my family really made the difference." Bud reached across from horseback to horseback and pulled Noah toward him, hugging his neck and kissing him on the check. "I love you Noah. You've always held a big place in my heart, Chief. I knew you were special, I just never knew how much."

Noah blushed, returning his grandfather's hug. "I love you too, Bud. I appreciate everything you ever done for me. I'm proud to have been your grandson on the other side, and I'm even more proud to be your Heavenly brother on this side. You left a good witness, and the Bible says that a righteous man leaves an inheritance for his children's children. I guess that inheritance is mine."

"And mine," Kelsie said, reaching for Noah's hand. "If it weren't for Noah, I wouldn't be here right now. I don't regret it either. I know life was short on the other side, but it was good. God gave me a short time with a good, Christian man over there and I've got an eternity to look forward to with him over here."

"Give God the glory for it all," Bud replied. "We all muddle through life the best we know how. But He's the one that made us, made a place for us, and made a way for us."

Joe shot a glance at his uncle. "If I didn't know better, Bud, I'd think you were about to preach."

Bud chuckled and said, "Well Joe, I thought a time or two that I might have been good at it, but I figure God never called me, 'cause I wouldn't have known when to shut up."

"Well Bud, it looks like this would be as good a time as any," Slim replied wryly. "Here comes Noah's brother, and it looks like he's a man on a mission."

As the group followed Slim's line of sight, they saw Benjamin walking from the within the city toward them, dressed once again in the white robes of an Emissary. Noah hoisted himself off the rail of the fence and hugged his brother as he approached. "Well, we did it, Ben. Mission accomplished," he said with a grin.

Benjamin nodded, smiling. "Yes, you certainly did," he said, looking around at the herd of horses milling into the stables. "And right on time. You and the rest of the riders are supposed to report to The Thrones. There is an important event about to take place, and your trail drive has been just one small part of it."

Noah gave him a knowing look. "I think I can imagine where this is going. If it's what I think it is, I can't wait."

A moment of brotherly intuition passed between them and Benjamin's gaze was inscrutable as ever, but there was a ghost of a twinkle in his dark eyes. "You may have a pretty good idea."

The group of one hundred and forty four riders set out for The Thrones, situated in the center of New Jerusalem. They left their horses at the stables, since the pace of the city was more suited to foot traffic. As Kelsie and Noah walked along together, they enjoyed the sights and sounds of this portion of the city, through which they had never traveled. As grand in scope and size as New Jerusalem was, they knew that a tour lasting ten thousand years wouldn't allow them to see it all. Thankfully, they had much more time than that.

As they walked, Kelsie held Noah's hand. Turning to him she said, "Noah, when we get finished with whatever God has for us, can we go back home and just rest? I've really enjoyed this, but I want to take a break for about, oh, a thousand years or so and just enjoy our home. We built it together, and I love it. I can't wait to get back."

Noah put his arm around her shoulder and pulled her close, kissing her hair lightly, drinking up its fragrance. "Sounds like someone's nesting instincts are kicking in. I want to get back too. But it may be a while, Kelsie. If I'm right, we're not done, not by a long shot."

Kelsie looked at him. "I wish you would tell me what you're thinking. You've been all mysterious about this ever since we started out for King's Canyon."

Noah nodded thoughtfully. "I know, but I want to be sure my assumptions are right. If they are, you are going to love what's about to happen. Then, when we are finished, we can go home and kick off our shoes for ten thousand years if you like. We can plant that orchard you mentioned, and I can build a studio for music and art."

"Can we finally get some cows?" Kelsie said suddenly, with a childlike excitement in her eyes. "You have been promising me cows ever since we met. So far . . . no cows. What's the deal, Noah? You trying to hold out on me?"

Noah laughed a good long, hearty laugh. "I *promise*," he said with great emphasis, bowing as he did so, "I will get you some cows; all the cows you want. A mighty thundering herd of cattle."

"Eh, I don't need a mighty thundering herd. I just want some cows; black and white ones, preferably," she said, satisfied with his answer.

As they neared the hub of the city, Noah and Kelsie noted that a wide channel of crystal clear water remarkably like the River of Life they had seen earlier ran alongside the Asher Road. Noah turned to Benjamin who walked along with them and asked about it. "What river is this? It can't be the River of Life. It runs between Judah and Rueben."

Benjamin shook his head and smiled. "Actually, the River of Life runs between every major highway of New Jerusalem. The streams of the River of Life begin at the pool of The Thrones and spread out in twelve different branches, like spokes of a wheel, watering the entire city. The highways also form twelve spokes, coming from the same hub, reaching outward to the gates of the city."

"Like a wheel within a wheel," Noah said with a sudden revelation showing in his eyes. "That makes total sense."

"What do you mean that?" Kelsie asked, looking at him.

Noah explained. "When Ezekiel was having all those wild visions, he saw what he described as a 'wheel within a wheel' in the sky. People have speculated that it was everything from angels, to flying saucers. But now I suspect he was seeing the layout of New Jerusalem."

Benjamin grinned. "Well eventually, you're bound to bump into him around here. When that happens, you'll just have to ask him."

CHAPTER THIRTY EIGHT

A
s the group of one hundred and forty four pressed toward the center of the city, making their way to The Thrones, they noticed that the foot traffic coming from the city's hub was much heavier than the traffic leading to it. Likewise, angels had been posted at major intersections, to direct foot traffic and help sustain order. Something was definitely going on, and Noah determined to find out what it was.

He spotted a large angel with the gold toned skin and almond shaped eyes. The angel had his hair pulled back in one long straight braid that hung to his waist. Noah approached him and as he did so, the angel turned to him and said, "I'm sorry son of man, but you are encouraged to enjoy the outer portions of New Jerusalem at this time. The center of the city is being cleared for a special event."

Noah nodded with acknowledgment. "I understand, but my friends and I have been summoned to The Thrones."

Now the angel turned to look at him intently and gazed for a moment at the troop of travelers with him. "Are you one of the groups of one hundred and forty four?" he queried.

One of the groups? Noah wondered to himself. *There was more than one? How many are there?* Aloud, he answered the angel. "Yes, there are a hundred and forty four of us."

"Then you have returned from a completed mission," the angel replied. "Please, go your way. Jehovah Yahweh and Jesus Christ are expecting you. May the Father of all of us bless you and your group." He bowed a slight bow of respect.

Noah returned the gesture and motioned for the rest. "Come on!" he called. "We need to get there."

As they came into the radiant light that shown from vast courtyard of The Thrones, the group began to pluck the succulent ripe fruit that hung plentifully from the groves of the Tree of Life that grew along the banks of the river. As they consumed the fruit, they felt the vibrant life and restoration of the land soak into the fiber of their being. Even though they had not been fatigued in the least by the journey and the mission they had undertaken, they still felt refreshed and rejuvenated by the fruit and the experience. Every bite was like being washed in waters of the River of Life.

Throughout the history of man, many had sought to find some elusive fountain of youth, some key to immortality. But the fact was that man had once been given free access, only to lose it by disobedience. Now, here it was in abundance, in such close proximity to the presence of the Creator, that it almost seemed to be merely an after thought. As amazing as this experience was, none lingered among the groves of the Tree of Life, when The Thrones of God lay directly ahead.

As they reached the courtyard covered many square miles, the entire group could tell that something big was happening. On either side of The Thrones, there were twelve smaller seats in a row, twenty four in all. Seated on one side were the patriarchs of the twelve tribes of Israel, for whom the gates and streets of the city had been named. Across from them sat twelve men who were obviously the twelve Apostles, whose names were written on the foundations of New Jerusalem. These two groups made up the twenty four elders that John had envisioned while in a trance on the isle of Patmos nearly two thousand years ago.

Directly in front of The Thrones, sitting as an audience some distance from the dais, were several thousand men and women that had been significant laborers in the faith throughout history. Prophets, judges, kings and priests from throughout the Bible were seated there. Martyrs who had died throughout human history for the truth of the gospel of Christ were there.

Abraham of Ur sat in awestruck wonder with the promised descendants of his simple faltering faith, with a legacy that stretched through thousands of years of human existence. Noah . . . the original

Noah, the raving, dreaming boat builder that would have been labeled a lunatic in any generation, sat fulfilled by the knowledge that His Creator, the one that sat before him, had used him to save nearly all those that were here today. Moses looked in abject adoration on the face of his God; the One that he had once seen only in passing and longed to see face to face for the rest of his life.

Mary was there, beaming at the One that had once, for a very short time, been her earthly son, who was now her Redeemer and her God. John the Baptist, no longer dressed in rough camel's hair, but in fine linen, knelt, and raised both hands to the One that he had once proclaimed to be the Lamb of God. Polycarp of Smyrna, Ignatius of Antioch and Clement of Rome were rapt by the image of the One whom they had believed in when being a follower of Christ was a fledgling, heretical, and deadly lifestyle. They had died a martyr's death; now they enjoyed an eternal life.

Then Noah looked to the perimeter of the courtyard and saw them. Surrounding those seated before The Thrones were groups like his own; knots of individuals, standing together, bonded together some task they had performed together as a mission. Like the group that had been on the trail drive, each gathering seemed to be a cross section of humanity and history, called together to complete some work that Jehovah Yahweh had deemed important.

Sensing a presence on either side of him, Noah felt Kelsie take his right hand, while another person took his left. He gave Kelsie's hand a little squeeze and turned to his left to find that the one who had taken his hand was his brother Benjamin. "Tell me," Noah said, as if Benjamin should know the questions in his mind; and as it happened, Benjamin did.

"You are wondering what the meaning of this is, and what the purposes of these other groups assembled were. I cannot tell you why we are gathered here, but I can tell you that there has never been a gathering like this before. But I have my thoughts about the matter; no human or angel know the day or the hour, but the signs are not difficult to see. As for the other groups, they were called to accomplish other missions for The King. Your hundred and forty four were asked to bring the King's horses; another was called to plant His vineyard; still others to build mansions, forge millions of new swords, make as many new stones." Noah fingered the small white inscribed stone hanging around his neck.

"In all, a thousand such groups were called up," Benjamin continued. "A thousand bands of one hundred and forty four each, called to accomplish a task. There are one hundred and forty four thousand servants in all. They have all completed their mission. The exquisite home that The Lamb has prepared for His bride appears complete. I expect we have been called here as wedding guests."

"Wedding guests?" Kelsie said in a puzzled tone. "I thought there weren't any weddings in Heaven."

"Only one," Noah replied, looking at her with a smile in his eyes. "Jesus and the church, referred to as His bride. The way I seem to remember Dad explaining it, ancient traditional weddings didn't happen until the groom got the house ready for his bride. When the groom was finished, he would ask his father to inspect the home. If everything was in order, he would give his son permission to go get his bride and bring her home for the wedding feast."

Kelsie's eyes were bright with excitement. "Does that mean what I think it does?"

"Is sure hope so," Noah replied. "I'd love to see the rest of our families and friends."

Just as he spoke, Benjamin gripped Noah's arm and got his attention. Nodding toward The Thrones, he indicated that they should be silent; something was about to happen.

Jehovah Yahweh looked about the courtyard at the assembled subjects, His smile radiant upon His children. His voice was like the sound of all the waves of all the oceans crashed at once:

WELCOME MY GOOD AND FAITHFUL SERVANTS. YOU HAVE DONE VERY WELL. YOU HAVE BEEN FAITHFUL OVER A

FEW THINGS YOU HAVE BEEN GIVEN RESPONSIBILITY FOR. NOW, I WILL GIVE YOU RESPONSIBILITY OVER MANY THINGS. YOU ARE A NATION OF KINGS AND PRIESTS. YOU ARE MY CHILDREN AND I LOVE YOU VERY MUCH. YOU HAVE BEEN A SERVICE TO THE LAMB AND YOU HAVE HELPED HIM PREPARE THE HOME OF THE BRIDE. I HAVE LOOKED UPON IT, AND IT IS VERY GOOD.

Then, The Creator of all things turned and took the hand of His Son, looking lovingly into His eyes. He spoke once more:

IT IS TIME, SON. THE MARRIAGE SUPPER IS READY, THE BRIDAL PALACE IS PREPARED. YOU MAY GO GET THE CHURCH.

The Lamb of God kissed His Father's hand briefly, gazed around at the thousands of angels and humans staring at Him in rapt expectation. He released The Father's hand, stood up from the Throne, and with a deep peal of thunder that was heard all the way from Heaven to the other side, Jesus Christ abruptly disappeared.

CHAPTER THIRTY NINE

s Jesus Christ stood and vanished, two things happened in quick succession. The first thing was the collective gasp from all of Heaven. Every being throughout the land, from the heart of New Jerusalem to the peaks of the mountain ranges that ringed the vast landscape knew it; felt it in the depth of their heart when Jesus left the realm of Heaven. The effect was one of something akin to a spiritual *brownout*; although God the Father remained on His Throne, the Light of the land had stepped back into the other side. The effect could not be escaped. There was a moment where all the citizens of Heaven felt a flash of emotion that seemed totally foreign, yet vaguely familiar from their time on the other side. It was a hint of the feeling of being alone.

Fortunately, the second thing that occurred happened so quickly that Heaven's citizens scarcely had time to register the emptiness in their heart. Jehovah Yahweh raised his hands and made a gentle sweeping gesture, as He spoke words that penetrated the hearts and minds of every human, every angel and every creature in Heaven. It was a simple, yet effective phrase, once spoken by a carpenter and itinerant preacher millennia ago.

"PEACE ... BE STILL."

The effect was immediate; the same breath that formed a mighty collective gasp, exhaled in a corporate sigh of relief. All those years ago, when Jesus stood upon the bow of a small ship in the midst of a storm with a ragtag group of followers, He had spoken those words; and He had calmed not only the storm around them, but the fearful men in the boat. Now the Father employed the same tactic on a much grander scale, calming the fears and doubts in the hearts of every being within His Kingdom.

What was left was a stillness unlike anything anyone in Heaven had ever experienced. There was a hush that literally could be felt from mountain range to mountain range. All music had ceased; all lively discussions, sounds of labor—everything was utterly silent. Everyone in Heaven, both in the city of New Jerusalem and in the surrounding twelve lands were completely silent. Even the seraphim at The Thrones ceased their vocal praises. As the quiet became tangible, every angel, every human, everything that had breath knew what was taking place. Only once since the dawn of time had Jesus Christ left The Thrones . . . and now, He was gone again.

Noah and Kelsie looked at each other in electric anticipation. For the first time since they had arrived in Heaven, they sensed something they thought they had left behind on the other side forever; they felt the passing of time. Moments ticked away, as all stood waiting for Christ's return. But surprisingly, the mood was not foreboding. In fact, it was one of excitement. The best way to describe it was something akin to waiting in silence for someone to walk through the door at a surprise celebration. The focus was not on the preparations, the event, or the joy to come; the focus was on the *arrival.*

One minute became five; five became fifteen. Time marched into Heaven like an invading army. It was an event as alien to Heaven as it had been on the other side when God had turned back the sun for Hezekiah in the book of Isaiah. Time had never encroached in this place; but this was different. It was as if some great mute stopwatch had been started.

As the time approached a half an hour, a deep, primal trembling began to shake the very foundations of Heaven itself. The vibration became a rumbling that grew louder with each passing second. With the sound came an increase in luminescence; the air itself seemed to grow brighter and crisper. The visibility of their surroundings became even more distinct. It was as if someone was turning a giant rheostat, increasing the volume, the light, the energy of all things Holy and Heavenly cranked to a maximum gain.

Suddenly, a lightning bolt filled the sky over New Jerusalem and struck The Thrones with a mighty clap of thunder that was even greater than the one that had occurred thirty minutes earlier. There was a blinding flash of light, as if a star had exploded in a dazzling supernova.

For a brief moment, no one could see anything, but it was obvious that something magnificent had occurred. As soon as the lightning flashed,

Noah and Kelsie felt the presence of The One who had left. The Lamb of God had returned, but there was something else; the presence of many, many others.

When the aurora of that brilliant flash faded, Jesus stood in front of The Thrones, and the expansive courtyard was filled to capacity with a very stunned multitude of people. The press of humanity extended to the perimeter of the courtyard and beyond, as millions of shocked people found themselves transported in an instant from the other side into the city of New Jerusalem.

Kelsie felt someone suddenly standing right beside her, and turned to find a slack jawed, wide eyed woman from China, staring at The Thrones and all those around her in utter amazement. On an impulse, she gave her a hug and a kiss on the cheek. "Welcome to Heaven!" she said with an enthusiastic smile in flawless Mandarin. "You made it!"

As the reality of what had just occurred began to sink in, Jesus Christ addressed the massive crowd.

I AM ALPHA AND OMEGA, THE BEGINNING AND THE END. I WILL GIVE UNTO YOU THAT ARE THIRSTY FROM THE FOUNTAIN OF THE WATER OF LIFE FREELY. BEHOLD, THE TABERNACLE OF GOD IS WITH HUMANITY, AND I WILL DWELL WITH YOU, AND YOU SHALL BE MY PEOPLE, AND GOD HIMSELF SHALL BE WITH YOU, AND BE YOUR GOD.

YOUR TEARS HAVE BEEN WIPED AWAY. THERE SHALL BE NO MORE DEATH, NEITHER SORROW, NOR CRYING, NEITHER SHALL THERE BE ANY MORE PAIN: FOR THE FORMER THINGS ARE PASSED AWAY. BEHOLD I MAKE ALL THINGS NEW. YOU HAVE INHERITED ALL THINGS; AND I WILL BE YOUR GOD, AND YOU SHALL BE MY CHILDREN. *(Revelation 21:3-7, ESV, Paraphrased)*

At the sound of His voice, every soul in the courtyard fell to their knees. Millions that had been at work, sleep, rest or play were now at worship. Those that had suffered now suffered no more. Maimed individuals raised new arms and hands to in praise to the Creator of the universe. Everyone from the arthritic to the paralytic felt the immediate and total healing of their bodies. The mute cried out with wondrous new words of praise and those that were blind since birth saw Jesus for the first time they saw anything. The joy was overwhelming; the entire city was awash with praise, worship, and thanksgiving on a scale far grander than imaginable.

The worship continued until finally Jesus gestured to a figure down front, close to The Thrones. The man rose, and Christ reached out, helping him step up on the dais so he could address the multitude. The man had unique, exotic features that seemed to be a mixture of every race of humanity. He was brown skinned, with dark curly hair and deep green eyes. As Jesus nodded to him, the man began to speak.

"I am Adam," he began, "the father of your race. I am honored and humbled to speak to you and to welcome you all to New Jerusalem. As you might have surmised, you have just experienced what you may have referred to as 'The Rapture', or 'The catching away of the Saints'. Here we call it the Marriage Supper of the Lamb, for you, as the Bride of Christ, have been brought to the home prepared for you by your Savior and King. In the Biblical book of John, Jesus said, 'I go to prepare a place for you.' (John 14:2, KJV) This is that place of which He spoke. Give Him praise and glory!"

The crowd erupted with a cheer that mounted in waves, reverberating all the way to the outer walls of the city. After allowing them a few moments, Adam held up a hand to quiet the crowd, and then continued. "This is a glorious event for all of us. You are encouraged to enjoy all the joys and pleasures that await you here. New Jerusalem is a city with no parallel, and Heaven is truly a land beyond your wildest imagination. You will eventually have all the time you need for this, for time takes no toll upon this place or its citizens. That said, after a time of celebration, we ask you to please return to The Thrones. You will be called when it is time. There is yet work to be done."

"What does Adam mean by that?" Noah asked, turning to Benjamin. "There have been a hundred and forty four thousand of us working on getting things done. Our family is here somewhere," he said, putting his arm around Kelsie. "Both of our families are here . . . friends too. I want to find them; I want to see them." Kelsie nodded in agreement.

Benjamin put a calming hand on Noah's arm. "And you will have plenty of time for that," he said gently. "I want to see them too. I want to meet my sister and her family, see my mother and father. But this is just the beginning. When the Church was brought here, it started the clock on seven years of great tribulation for the other side. Terrible things will happen and many will die for the cause of Christ. There will be more people coming; refugees by the thousands. There are preparations to be made. We are at war, Noah. War with the enemy; Lucifer has not, and will not give up until the very end. So we still must take the battle to him. The calvary of Calvary must ride out with the King, and the Kingdom of God must be established on Earth, as it is in Heaven."

Kelsie exchanged a determined look with Noah. "So does that mean what I think it means?" she asked Benjamin.

"Yes," Benjamin replied. "It does. We have seven years to prepare and train with the soldiers of Heaven. In seven years, you will both see the other side again. In seven years, you're going back."

AFTERWORD

I hope you have enjoyed "The Last Great Adventure". It has been therapeutic for me and I hope it has been encouraging to some. When I first began this, I didn't know how long it would be, or what directions it would take. I had hoped it would be long enough to publish as a book, which I believe it is. Not one of these chapters has been written without tears and fond memories, and that's been good for me. I hope it's been good for you. Obviously, it is not the end; merely the beginning. There is ample room to continue this story, and I may, if the Lord is willing.

I know that some may question several things in this story, so I'll take the time to address a few areas that some may wonder about here. While I made some "disclaimers" in the introduction, I still think it's a good idea to mention these things.

Do you think this is what Heaven is really like? No, honestly, I think it is much better. I believe Heaven is real and that it is beyond our imagining. But a guy can dream can't he? I miss Noah, Kelsie, my father and a lot of others in this story and I really just want to think that they are enjoying life—and I really believe they are.

What about those of us that believe that we rest in the grave? I respect that view, and understand where it comes from. While I don't share it personally, if I find out that I'm wrong, I'm okay with that. That would just mean we all woke up at the same time, without any sense of lost years. I just took the view in this story I personally believe.

What about the Judgment? Personally, I believe the Judgment happens at the very end of time, and that those who are in Christ will already have their redemption established. I once saw a tract that depicted a man's judgment as standing before God, and having his past sins played on a screen for all to see. I find no evidence of that in the Bible, but I know that we are judged on our works and our names being written in the Book of Life. Since my works don't cut it, I'm relying on Jesus and the Book of Life. I don't believe that my sins will be played for all humanity, because God says they were cast into the depths of the sea, never more to be remembered.

Did you know that you got some of the events in the wrong order? The timeline of end times prophecy may be the most hotly debated subject in Christian theology. Ezekiel, Daniel, Matthew, The Revelation and several other books deal with this subject; the chronological order of the events mentioned is, "open to interpretation". We actually don't know and won't know for certain until the pieces fall into place. Also, while I've tried to be consistent to Biblical writings about Heaven, this is a work of fiction.

What if I don't believe Jesus is the only way to Heaven? Jesus said, "I am the way, the truth and the life." (John 14:6 KJV) He's not just A way, He is THE way. Fortunately, His "yoke is easy", meaning that it is not difficult to be a follower of Christ. Being a Christian makes your life easier, not harder, because you have God to lean on, and Heaven to look forward to. Obviously, it doesn't make it perfect; my family and I can attest to that. We've suffered many heartaches and trials, but the thing that helps is knowing that God is there to help us. He knows our troubles . . . and our weakness. He is always ready to help.

Thanks, and God bless. If I don't get to meet you here, please look me up when you get to New Jerusalem. I plan on being there.

CPSIA information can be obtained at www.ICGtesting.com
Printed in the USA
LVOW080419120613

338158LV00001B/4/P